TNTRIO Movement Book - 4

Franklin Ysaac + Eliseo Rio Jr. + Gus Guzman

April 2023

Content

oooooo

Preface

The main subject of this book and previous books is about results of the May 9, 2023 national elections in the Philippines.

A team of IT experts composed of the three(3) authors of these books have initiated moves to write about their findings and technical analyses of the election results.

The findings are well explained in many writings and postings in social media, particularly facebook, and the actions taken by them with the support of many sectors of society.

The updates had been recorded in previous books, published at amazondotcom, which are the following titles:

1-- Truth Petition to Comelec (Initial book)
2—Truth Warriors-1
3—Initial Stages of Truth Petition
4—Truth Warriors-2
5—Truth Patriots-1
6—Writ of Mandamus Petition
7—TNTrio Movement Book-1
8—TNTrio Movement Book-2
9—TNTrio Movement Book-3
10- TNTRIO Movement Book-4 (this one)

As this is a continuing movement, more books will be published from collection of writings and postings in the web to record all developments for posterity and guidance of all concerned.

oooooo

1
Guy Camacho – The Long Gray Line – Mar 2023

The hundreds of thousands who attended at every political rally organized for Leni Robredo were proofs that the 31 million Smartmatic count for BBM is a myth created by Comelec.

oooooo

2

Can Comelec explain why 60 million voted in 2022 vs 44 million

The total number of registered voters is only 44 Million during the previous national elections.

Paki-EXPLAIN nga ITO COMELEC Pls Lng?

The National Statistics office reports that the number of voters in the Philippines was posted at 43,331,229 persons or 56.64 percent of the total population.

The 2022 elections showed an unexplained increase of 60% casted votes or a total of 19 million more ballots reported who allegedly voted.
NSO/ COMELEC Registered
VOTERS = 44 Million
Actually read by smartmatic machines/unofficial = 61 million votes.
Over voted = 18 million extra.

Bob Blues Magoo @MagooBl... · 14h
TAMA NA
SOBRA NA
PEKE KA
PALITAN NA!

Bart Guingona @guingonabart · 1h
Why didn't lawyers' groups and all else supporting Leni raise a howl at the point when something this obvious was was happening? Have we normalized massive cheating? Comelec transmission logs kinukwestyon ng ilang eksperto

cnnphilippines.com
Comelec transmission logs kinukwestyon ng ilang eksperto

Ooooooo

3
I SUPPORT COL. OSWALD ODONO'S IMPEACHMENT MOVEMENT - Supporter

Last night, after hearing Gen. Eliseo Rio Jr.'s explanation of the election vote count irregularities and statistically improbable near constant ratios of vote results between the presidential candidates, I have become more convinced of the illegitimacy of Marcos Jr. and Sara as President and VP-elect.

The graphs presented by Gen. Rio of the Comelec data provide the proverbial "smoking gun" evidence of the criminal conspiracy to rig the election and defraud the Filipino people.

I stand behind Col. Odono's move to impeach the Comelec commissioners under whose watch the massive fraud took place.

Comelec's reticent attitude and piece-meal response to popular demands for information that sheds light on the observed election irregularities betray their malevolent intent to delay the uncovering of the truth, to keep the illegitimately elected in power for as long as possible, and to tire the Filipino people into accepting the fraudulent election results.

I call on all my fellow Filipinos to unite and support Col. Odono's impeachment movement.

ooooo

4
Unconfirmed Reports in USA about Phil Elections of 2022 - Alda Gaño with Mildred Manaug

Not sure about veracity of this report - but just for your info:

Good Morning ALL, just talked to my cousin from US, per info, na hacked na raw ng US ang record/server ng comelec and found out na massive cheating ang nagyari, nag uumpisa ng mag ingay ang mga pinoy doon sa US, Canada and other part of america na ang true result na boto na nakuha ni Leni is 39M while BBM just got 14M. Nakialam na ang US sa imposibleng mangyari ang result na pinalabas nila, sa US & Canada, 70% nag vote kay Leni pero ang result, talo siya. Per my cousin, baka magka gulo due to this effect marami ng mga US marchalls ang naka position sa ibat ibang lugar ng pinas including sa comelec waiting for order. IOn senatorial race, No 1 is Delima and No 2 si Trillanes. Ang resultang pinalabas ng comelec is bogus at ang pandaraya nasa mismong server na kahit kanino ng name ang ilagay ang output is always BBM & Sarah. Imagine, 39M si Leni as compared to BBM na 14M lang. Kalat na eto sa US and nag uumpisa na ang mga protesta, kaya nga unti unti ng nagpu pull out ng mga investment ang US sa pag kakaupo ni BBM, it's gonna be hell. Again this came from my reliable source sa US and lahat na info na nakukuha ko is talagang nangyayari just like what I mentioned before na a month ago pa, gawa na ang resulta. Sana lumabas na ang totoong resulta

Ikalat po natin eto para lumabas na ang totoo.
Salamat po.

Not sure about veracity of this report - but just for your info:

Good Morning ALL, just talked to my cousin from US, per info, the US has hacked the record/server of comelec and found out that massive cheating happened, Filipinos are starting to make noise in US, Canada and other parts of America that are true The result of the votes that Leni got is 39M while BBM just got 14M. The US has intervened in the impossible of the result that they released, in the US & Canada, 70% voted for Leni but the result is, she lost. Per my cousin, there might be chaos due to this effect many US marshalls are in position in different places of the Philippines including comelec waiting for order. Ion senatorial race, No 1 is Delima and No 2 is Trillanes. The result released by comelec is bogus and the fraud is in the server itself that whoever's name is put the output is always BBM & Sarah. Imagine, 39M si Leni compared to BBM na 14M only. It's already spread in the US and the protests are starting, that's why the US is slowly pulling out investments in BBM's sitting, it's gonna be hell. Again this came from my reliable source in the US and all the info that I get is really happening just like what I mentioned before that a month ago, the result is already made. Hope the real result will come out soon

Let's spread this so the truth will come out.

Salamat po.

OOOOOO

5
Army of Truth Seekers -This is the truth – March 2023

Nagkaroon lang talaga ng malawakang pagmamaniobra sa resulta dahil yung kapatid niyang babae ang namumuno sa committee. At sinunog na ang ebidensya at pinapatahimik ang mga kakunchaba. Reflection yan ng umatend ng irigasyon niya, este inagurasyon daw na wala man lagpas tatlong libo ang dumalo. At mga concert nung umawit ng ako'y pilipino at cancelled concert ni humanap ng anghit. Katakataka na hindi man nagreflect sa actual na mga election rally nila ang sinasabe nilang 31M. Pag panahon talaga ng pagnanakaw at pandaraya eh panahon talaga. Pag panahon ng totoo at tama eh talagang panahon talaga. Magsaya muna sila kase panahon nila. Pero hindi obob ang Pilipinas. Nagmamatchag at nagmamasid lang sa ngayon. Pero nagbabantay ang mga nasa tama at totoo

#TROLLBusters
#STOPPoliticalTrollMachinery
#ArmyOfTrollSeekers #TRUTHFarm
#TruthFactsRecords
#SOCMEDpaTROLL
#FBpaTROLL
#PHYouthnited2022
#PHUnited2022
#AOTSteam

This is the truth !

There was only extensive maneuvering in the result because it was her sister who was leading the committee. And the evidence has been burned and the cowards are silenced. That's a reflection of the one who attended his irrigation, I mean, it was an inauguration that no more than three thousand attended. And the concerts when they sang "I am a Filipino" and the canceled concert of Manap Nghit. It's strange that the 31M did not reflect on their actual election rally. When it's time of stealing and cheating, it's really time. When the time is true and right, it's really the time. Let them have fun because it's their time. But the Philippines is not stupid. Just checking and observing so far. But those who are right and true are watching !

> #TROLLBusters
> #STOPPoliticalTrollMachinery
> #ArmyOfTrollSeekers #TRUTHFarm
> #TruthFactsRecords
> #SOCMEDpaTROLL
> #FBpaTROLL
> #PHYouthnited2022
> #PHUnited2022
> #AOTSteam

oooooo

6

AFP is not Duterte or Marcos Army – Doan Azarias
March 2023

IT IS NOT DUTERTE'S OR MARCOS JR.'S PRIVATE ARMY.

THE ARMED FORCES OF THE PHILIPPINES (AFP) MUST NOT SHIRK ITS CONSTITUTIONAL RESPONSIBILITIES THAT IT IS SWORN TO.

THE MILITARY GENERALS MUST LEAD THE

COUNTRY'S ARMIES TO DEFEND THE COUNTRY'S DEMOCRATIC SYSTEM OF GOVERNMENT AND THE CONSTITUTIONAL RIGHTS OF THE FILIPINO PEOPLE.

IT'S AN OUTRAGE THAT THE AFP DID NOT EVEN LIFT A FINGER TO TOPPLE THE PREVIOUS REPRESSIVE REGIME UNDER DUTERTE. AND IT IS AN INDIGNATION THAT IT IS OPENLY DISPLAYING ITS SUBSERVIENCE TO THE NEW REGIME UNDER MARCOS JR. THAT WAS ILLEGALLY INSTALLED WITH THE COMELEC'S HELP AND THROUGH MACHINATED SD CARDS AND VCMS.

DUTERTE HAD MOCKED AND DEMEANED THOSE MILITARY GENERALS BY PUBLICLY BLURTING, TIME AND TIME AGAIN, THAT HE WAS FEEDING THEM WITH MONEY - TAXPAYERS' MONEY AND PUBLIC FUNDS - THAT HE PLUNDERED FROM THE COUNTRY'S COFFERS. AND REGRETTABLY, THOSE GENERALS TOOK IT LYING DOWN AND DIDN'T PUSH BACK AND THUS, GIVING CREDENCE TO DUTERTE'S CLAIM.

Wake up, you PMA generals, shame on you for not standing up to defend your honors and moral principles. You are Constitutionally organized and not Duterte's and Marcos Jr.'s private army.

Do your Constitutionally-mandated job by defending and protecting the country's sovereignty and the security and well-being of the Filipino people.

Step up and overthrow those bastards who are prostituting the Motherland!

Don Azarias

☐

Comments:

Tess Nayles

a shame to the generals ! generals,,,! prove him he's lying(d dutertard)

Jean Langcayas

Some are blinded by promises and pledges ,but there are those who stand in what theyve pledged to the people,,to serve and protect,, we need the repeat performance of those Patriots in uniforms ,,

"PINAKAIN KO NG PERA ANG MGA GENERAL!" --- DF PRES. DUTERTE

THE statement of Duterte that he fed the Generals and that the General's stomachs are full — is very very alarming to both gov't officials and the citizens. It is revolting! The Generals, being graduates from the PMA, and schooled in the best and finest tradition of God, honor and love for country, should all stand up and deny the shameful statement of Rodrigo Duterte and demand for an apology; that is, if the Generals still value the meaning of God, honor and love of country.

Unfortunately, as it is, it appears that the Generals may indeed have been bribed to the fullest by Duterte. Otherwise, with the word "HONOR" in their minds, they will not tolerate this INSULT and humiliation leveled against them before the world community.

DJ PRESIDENT RAGEN LAO PAMATONG

oooooo

7
Cheaters - People Will judge You - Darius Balosa

Kapag napatunayang dinaya nyo ang Taong Bayan. Taong Bayan din ang hahatol sa inyo! #CTTOphoto

When proven that you cheated the People. The people of the country will also judge you! #CTTOphoto

oooooo

8

Let the transmission logs come out via People's Mandamus Petition for this purpose
Franklin Ysaac

Thank you to all our truth supporters and followers

For info, this people's mandamus is not the same as the first change org petition last year . In the first petition, we reached more than 70k signatures .

This people's mandamus is the fastest rally of our signature campaign . At the rate the signatures are coming in, we may hit not only 500,000 but 1,000,000.00 before the anniversary of the May 9 election debacle .

Pray that we hit this number as we will attach this to our mandamus petition before the Supreme Court .

So Comelec, you have been notified by the overwhelming disenfranchised voters with their signatures who are now calling out for truth and transparency.

Let the true transmission logs come out and let the people know the whole truth and nothing but the truth.

This is screenshot of the latest update and the tally is increasing by leaps and bounds.

oooooo

9
Why China Interferes in Philippine 2022 Election
Perry Talledo – April 1, 1023

Perry Natividad Talledo – April 1, 2023

WHY & HOW CHINA SECRETLY INTERFERES IN PHILIPPINE ELECTION 2022 INORDER TO IN ABLE BONGBONG MARCOS (friend of China) TO WIN AS PRESIDENT INSPITE OF LENI ROBREDO's OVER WHELMING SUPPORT BY THE FILIPINO PEOPLE

Some 20,000,000 votes for Bongbong were secretly transmited to ELECTION CENTRAL SERVER (Manila) on the first hour of canvassing (7:00 PM MAY 9, 2022) .... This is the photo of one of the islands (Spratly Island) in WEST PHILIPPINE SEA that secretly transmitted Marcos votes.

ANG TAMANG SAGOT KUNG BAKIT NANGHIHIMASOK ANG CHINA SA HALALAN SA PILIPINAS.

ANALYSIS (ISANG PAGSISIYASAT)

Exactly after 7:05 pm on May 9, 2022 after the closing of voting & all presincts closed , COMELEC recieved Secret transmission of 20 million votes from an island controled by CHINA in the WEST PHILIPPINE SEA. Presumably unknown to all Filipinos COMELEC higher-ups made secret deals and links with the outside source of this secret transmission by revealing to them the TOTAL VOTES tallied by VCM's in more than 126,000 presincts all over the country. It is apt for these outside contacts to manipulate the results of Philippine votes. The outside Chinese technology source sent the 20 million votes in the first hour of counting and would be ofcourse an advance votes for BONGBONG MARCOS which would then be very difficult for Leni Robredo's votes to catch-up even though in the succeeding hours of counting of the remaining precincts still to be oounted... and then release their OWN ELECTION RETURNSTO CENTRAL SERVER IN MANILA. In other words, nakalamang na sina BONGBONG ng 20 million votes over his presidential contender LENI ROBREDO.

(SALIN SA WIKANG TAGALOG) .....

Walang naka-alam na mga Pilipino maliban sa matatas na pinono (Chairmans) na mayroon pala kasundaan ang COMELEC chairmans sa isa sa mga CHINESE COMPUTER STATIONS doon sa isa sa isla sa WEST PHILIPPINE SEA (sa bakuran lang ng Pilipinas). Itong kasunduan sa mga Chinese ay napag-usapan na nina BONGBONG MARCOS, ang humahangad na manalo sa halalan kahit sa sa ano mang masamang paraan ang BUMISITA SIYA SA EMBAHADA NG TSINA BAGO DUMATING ANG ARAW NGHALALAN......

Pinagsusuri ngayon ng TNT TRIO (Ginoong ELISEO RIO JR. Ginoong FRANKLIN YSAAC, at Ginoong GUS LAGMAN) – ang tinuturing COMPUTER TECHNOLOGY EXPERTS NG PILIPINAS ang isang kababalaghan (Mystery) kung saan nagagaling ang 20 million votes na pinadala sa Central Server COMELEC sa Manila at sino ang nagpadala sa luob lang ng isang horas. (The Science of Politics: PNTALLEDO - Netherlands)

• **Cecilia San Diego**
Wow. Love this news

Nod Alayar
Bayan Ko
"31M DID NOT VOTE for BBM-Sara. . . . . .".
The word is out and loud.
Such palpable and pervasive belief will always come to bear unless and until an honest and impartial

investigation uncovers the veracity of facts or fraud, truth or lies.

Election cheating and manipulation have been the practice for over a half century, in ever-escalating intensity and impunity. Therefore, the inevitable should not come as a complete surprise. And now the unthinkable and the incredulity of it just seemed to have transpired before our eyes. The majority is dumbfounded and helpless, it is totally outrageous.

The electoral process is supposed to harness the best potential and herald the future of the nation and the prosperity of its people.

The power-hungry who wins via fraud is a selfish pseudo-leader. Being illegitimate, he will follow the principles of Machiavelli to stay in power and surround himself with sycophants and opportunists.

He can never provide the elusive dreams of the people.

Dennis Uy's Vote Counting Machines are ALLEGED to have produced the FAKE 31M votes.

It is PATENTLY WRONG for COMELEC and Congress to lend credence to numbers provided by the RIGGED VCMs.

Election Recount of ACTUAL ballots at PRECINT level would have given REALISTIC and FACTUAL results.

BBM-Sara were certified as winners by COMELEC based on FRAUD & CHEATING through the VCMs of Dennis Uy.

FIGHT for our FUTURE NOW

or . . . . . THERE WILL be NOTHING MORE to FIGHT FOR.

Nod Alayar
Bayan Ko

The "Miting de Avance" or the Final Rally of Support nationwide on the last week prior to May National Election '22 was profoundly tell-tale. You couldn't possibly miss it or have any doubt as to the prospect of any other rational eventuality.

The massive attendance and exhuberant show of support was predictive of the peoples' choice.

The evening after the closure of voting activities was filled with optimistic anticipation. All these were fast eroding as the night wore on.

The morning after, ushered the most heart-crunching news of a political debacle.

The peoples' will was thwarted by a most insidious manipulation and machination.

A wanton and most devious form of wholesale betrayal of public trust. Utter and shameless political thievery in connivance with opportunists, enablers, sycophants and treasonous scum of society.

People Power is not enough, we need Divine Intervention.

oooooo

10

PEOPLE'S MANDAMUS PETITION
Mila Alvarez Magno

The TNTrio has prepared a "people's petition" on Change-org and is requesting all Filipinos who want to know the truth about the May 9 election irregularities to sign it.

The people's petition is designed to strengthen the Mandamus Petition that is now pending in the Supreme Court. It will be submitted as a supplementary manifestation to the Court.

The people's petition demands Comelec to preserve and release true transmission logs.

It is very worthy of your support.
PLEASE CLICK THIS LINK:
https://chng.it/79gg9SqWmq
and add your name to the list of signatories.
DO NOT CLICK THE LINK TO "CHIP IN" MONEY AS
THIS WILL GO TO THE CHANGE ORGANIZATION.
Quoting **Franklin Ysaac**:
"Mila Alvarez Magno this people's mandamus is initiative for people to make the same demand like what we filed sa SC . And total of this signature campaign will be added to our next supplemental petition. It's not contrary to our original mandamus . In fact it bolsters our petition as we have backing of people now."

oooooo

11
Comelec Deceives andConfuses the Public – Eliseo Rio Jr – TNTRIO member – April 2023

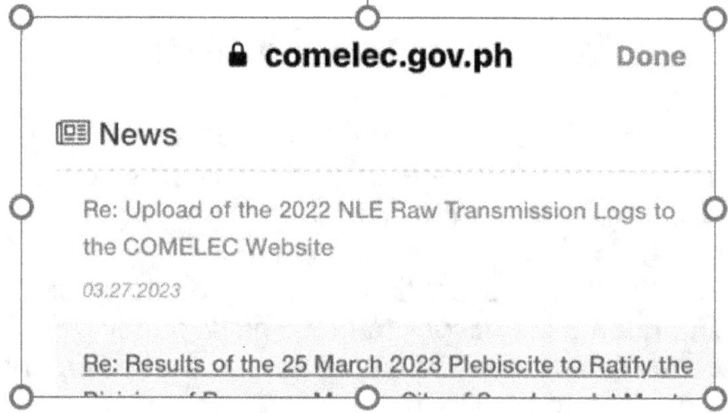

🔒 **comelec.gov.ph**   Done

Top Menu ▾

◉ COMELEC

List of VCM Received Transmission Logs May 9, 2022 NLE

Updated: 27 March 2023

- List of VCM Received During First Hour of Transmission May 9, 2022 NLE

- List of VCM Received Entire Transmission Logs May 9, 2022 NLE

- Raw File(s):

  - ⬇ logstrapc01srv01_2022-05-26-1441.tar.gz [67,961 KB]

  - ⬇ logstrapc01srv02_2022-05-26-1441.tar.gz [67,923 KB]

  - ⬇ logstrapc01srv03_2022-05-26-1441.tar.gz [67,859 KB]

  - ⬇ logstrapc01srv04_2022-05-26-1441.tar.gz [67,859 KB]

  - ⬇ hash.txt

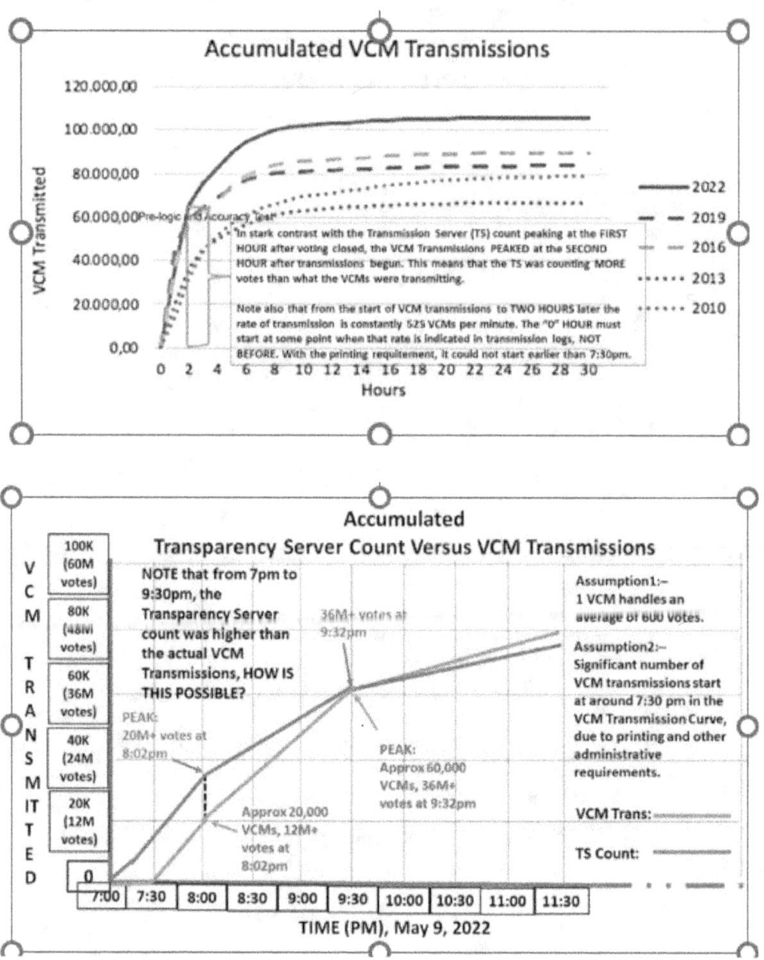

COMELEC is further deceiving the Public by confusing them. They publicly announced that COMELEC will show the Transmission Logs to prove that there were actually 20M+ votes transmitted by VCMs in the first hour after voting closed at 7pm on May 9, 2022. On March 23, 2023, COMELEC posted on its website the List of the 2022 NLE Raw Transmission Logs. When we pointed out to COMELEC that what they posted were NOT Transmission Logs of VCM transmissions but Reception Logs of the Server received data, they have now change their website to read "List of

VCM Received Transmission Logs May 9, 2022". How could there be a List of VCM Receive Transmission Logs? It is either VCM Transmission Logs or Server Reception Logs. These are two different lists. What was shown to the public are actually Server Reception Logs being mislabeled as Transmission Logs.

WHY CANNOT COMELEC JUST SHOW THE VCM TRANSMISSION LOGS THAT WAS THE BASIS OF THE "ACCUMULATED VCM TRANSMISSIONS" GRAPH THAT COMELEC SHOWED ON OCTOBER 18, 2022? It was clearly shown in that Graph the VCM transmissions PEAKED at the SECOND HOUR, in stark contrast with the Transparency Server received data that PEAKED at the FIRST HOUR after voting closed.

oooooo

12

THE COLLEGE DROPOUT WHO IS SPEAKING THROUGH HIS HAT - Don Azarias – April 2023

THEN HOW WERE YOU ABLE TO GET IN? IT'S EXACTLY YOU, YOURSELF, THAT YOU ARE TALKING ABOUT. AND DON'T FORGET IT WAS YOUR DICTATOR FATHER WHO STARTED IT ALL.

OF COURSE, THE FILIPINO PEOPLE KNOW HOW YOU - A COLLEGE DROPOUT - USED THE BILLIONS OF DOLLARS THAT YOUR FAMILY HAS PLUNDERED FROM THE COUNTRY'S COFFERS TO TRY TO REVISE AND SUPPRESS HISTORICAL FACTS BY HIDING THE VESTIGE OF THE MONSTROSITIES COMMITTED BY YOUR FATHER, WHO RULED THE COUNTRY - AND EVEN FALSELY CALLING IT THE

GOLDEN AGE - WITH IRON FIST, TO PERPETUATE HIMSELF IN POWER.

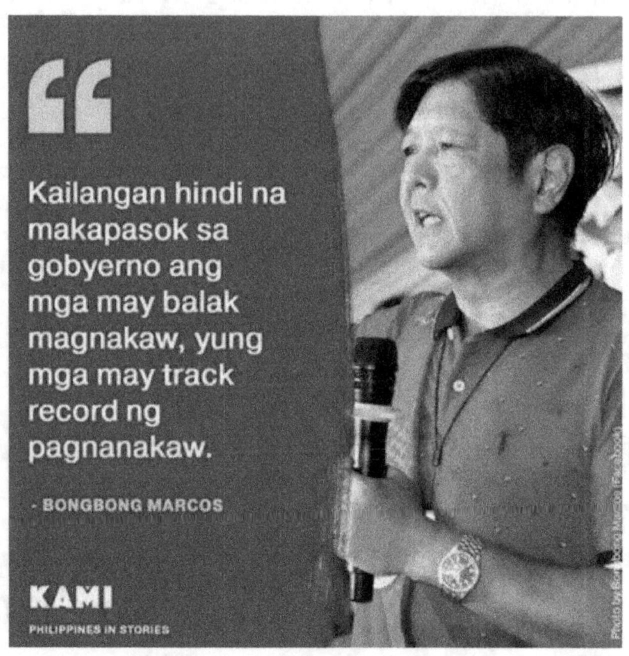

THEN WITH THE HELP OF DUTERTE, HIS POWERFUL ALLIES AND THE COMELEC ITSELF, YOU WERE CATAPULTED TO THE HIGHEST PUBLIC OFFICE THROUGH MACHINATED SD CARDS AND VCMS.

NOW THOSE INFO TECH EXPERTS AND HONEST PMA GENERALS AND MILITARY OFFICERS - WHO I BELIEVE WERE AWARE OF IT FROM THE VERY START - KNOW HOW YOU CHEATED YOUR WAY INTO THE PRESIDENCY.

HOW COULD YOU BLATANTLY USURP THE PRESIDENTIAL POWERS THAT DO NOT BELONG TO YOU AND SHOULD HAVE BELONGED TO LENI ROBREDO? ARE YOU THAT SHAMELESS AND INCORRIGIBLE?

Mr. Marcos Jr., please do the long-suffering Motherland and the Filipino people a favor: Please resign from the presidency that you don't have the right and moral compass to lead and just enjoy the $10 billion in taxpayers' money and public funds that your father stole from the country's coffers.

Will you?
Now!
Don Azarias

(Comments)
Jose Bernardo Lacson Jr.
BAKIT NANDYAN KA??

Teresita S. Escucha

Jean Celeste
Kapal nya talaga
Bunhuy Ajero Uy
Ha ha ha!!!!!! Alam na alam na ng buong mundo balong. Ikaw na lang hindi!!

Angie Samson
Look who's talking?.....Talk to yourself mr president😡😡😡😡

Raoul Navarro

Mind conditioning,playing unblemished and clean of any legal cases,that's if one is stupid and embicles to accept

"PINAKAIN KO NG PERA ANG MGA GENERAL!" --- DF PRES. DUTERTE

THE statement of Duterte that he fed the Generals and that the General's stomachs are full — is very very alarming to both govt officials and the citizens. It is revolting! The Generals, being graduates from the PMA, and schooled in the best and finest tradition of God, honor and love for country, should all stand up and deny the shameful statement of Rodrigo Duterte and demand for an apology; that is, if the Generals still value the meaning of God, honor and love of country.

Unfortunately, as it is, it appears that the Generals may indeed have been bribed to the fullest by Duterte. Otherwise, with the word "HONOR" in their minds, they will not tolerate this INSULT and humiliation leveled against them before the world community.

DJ PRESIDENT RAGEN LAO PAMATONG

oooooo

13
"Ang isda ay sa bibig nahuhuli." - Eliseo Rio Jr

COMELEC Spokesperson Atty John Rey Laudiangco clearly said that the "Accumulated VCM Transmissions" Graph shown to the public on October 18, 2022, PEAKED on the SECOND HOUR because COMELEC had improved the Automated Election System (AES).

SO HOW COME THE "Transmission Logs" COMELEC showed the public in its website on March 23, 2023 PEAKED at the FIRST HOUR?

Because these are NOT Transmission Logs BUT Reception Logs, whose data we are questioning, particularly the unbelievable PEAK 20M+ votes counted in the FIRST HOUR! COMELEC SHOULD show the public the Transmission Logs that were the basis of its own Graph shown on October 18, 2022, which Atty Laudiangco proudly proclaimed PEAKED at the

SECOND HOUR because COMELEC had became more efficient. If COMELEC will not do that, then it has become more efficient in deceiving the Filipino People.

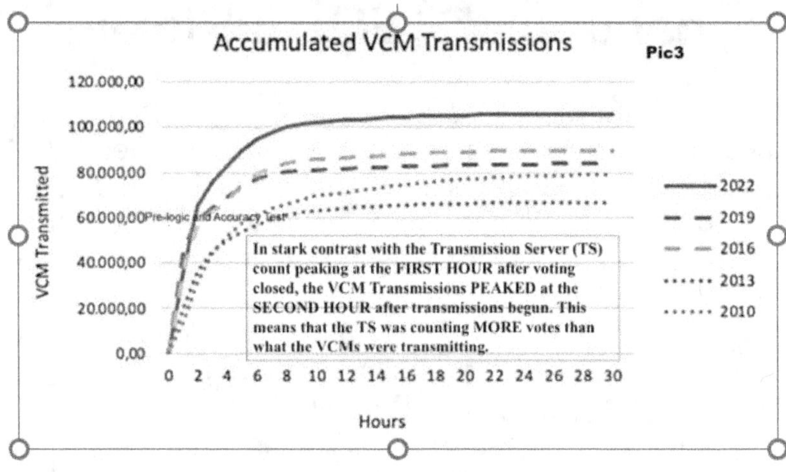

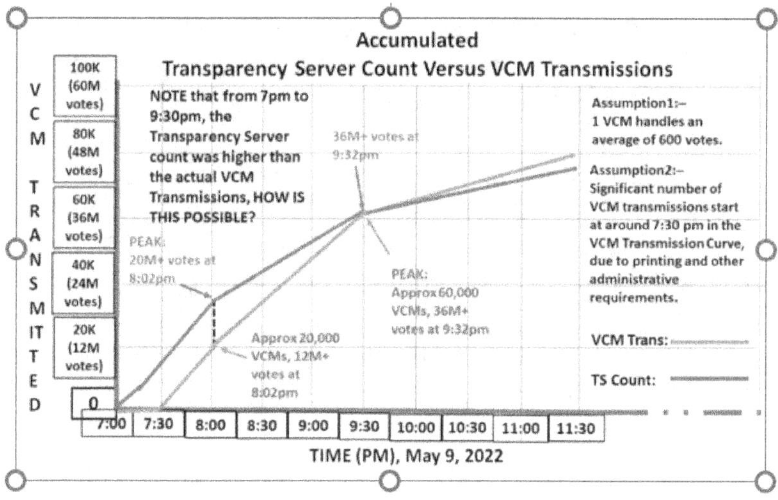

oooooo

14

HERE IS PROOF THAT COMELEC IS FOOLING THE FILIPINO PEOPLE:-
By Eliseo Rio Jr. (Ret) – Posted by Fred Santos at FB

The "Transmission Logs" shown by COMELEC to the public in its website are actually Reception Logs, being deceptively labeled by COMELEC in the media as Transmission Logs.

The first picture shows a Transmission Report of a VCM assigned to a clustered precinct located at Malanday Elementary School, Barangay Malanday, Marikina City, with Precinct ID 74020046. Note that the time of transmission was 20:05:04 of May 9, 2022.

On page 268 of the List of VCM Received on May 9, 2022, the VCM with Precinct ID 74020046 was the 40150th VCM to be received by the Server at 20:02:47 of May 9, 2022.

NOW, HOW COULD THE SERVER RECEIVE A VCM TRANSMISSION AROUND THREE (3) MINUTES BEFORE, REPEAT BEFORE, THE VCM ACTUALLY TRANSMITTED? Remember, this is just one of the 170,000 VCMs deployed during the May 9, 2022 Election, and many more of these anomalies will be discovered when compared with actual VCM Transmission Reports. No wonder COMELEC is NOT showing the VCM Transmission Logs and is duping the public by showing Reception Logs of the Servers.

PS. Time synchronization is an essential part of our Automated Election System (AES). All VCMs and Servers used in the AES are time synchronized, as the time in all smartphones and computers are synchronized when connected to the internet. That is why we never bother setting the time in our cellphones and computers, but the time in the cellphone or computer of someone besides you will have the same time as yours accurate to the hundredth of a second even if you both have different telco or ISP. All VCMs are time synchronized before they leave its central hub in Santa Rosa Laguna. In fact there is a big budget just to synchronize the VCM chronometers and subject them to a "Final Testing and Sealing of Vote Counting Machines" (FTSVCM) just before Election Day.

ooooooo

15
How can you refute or dispute this revelation? - Franklin Ysaac – April 2023

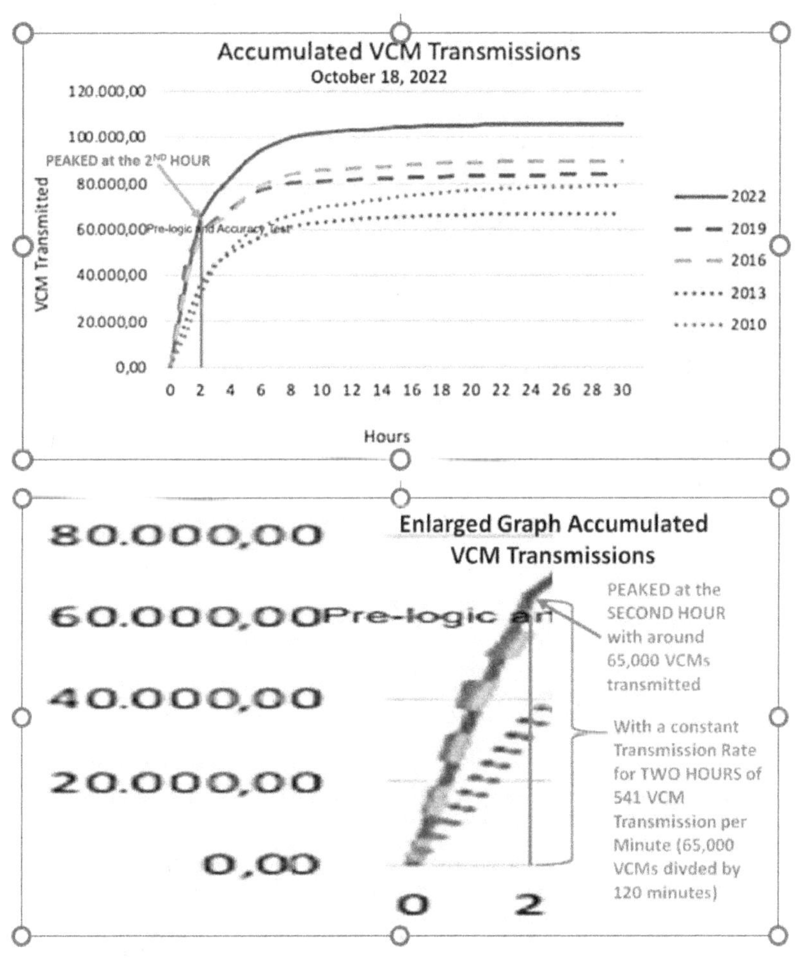

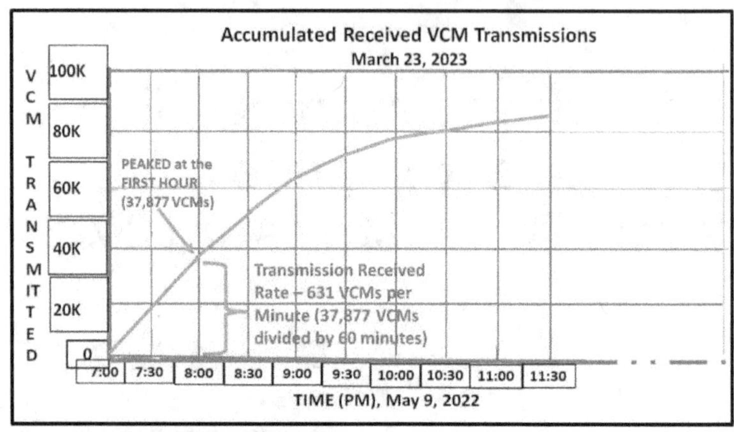

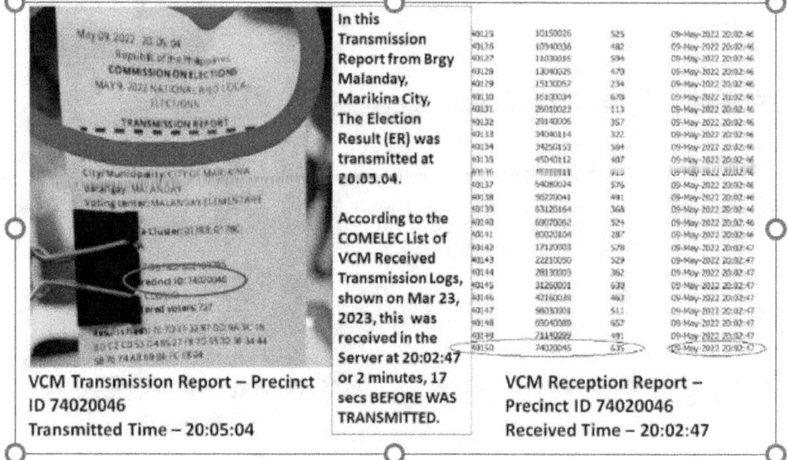

In this Transmission Report from Brgy Malanday, Marikina City, The Election Result (ER) was transmitted at 20.03.04.

According to the COMELEC List of VCM Received Transmission Logs, shown on Mar 23, 2023, this was received in the Server at 20:02:47 or 2 minutes, 17 secs BEFORE WAS TRANSMITTED.

VCM Transmission Report – Precinct ID 74020046
Transmitted Time – 20:05:04

VCM Reception Report – Precinct ID 74020046
Received Time – 20:02:47

oooooo

16
SIMPLE MATH AND LOGIC WILL PROVE THAT COMELEC MAY BE FOOLING THE FILIPINO PEOPLE. – Eliseo Rio Jr - 2023

On October 18, 2022, COMELEC showed the public a graph "Accumulated VCM Transmissions" which plotted the VCM Transmission Logs from start to finish in the 2022 Election. COMELEC Spokeperson Atty John Rex Laudiangco then proudly described the peaking of the VCM transmissions at the SECOND HOUR as the result of the "improvement in the Automated Election System (AES) and Servers". We noted that the SECOND HOUR PEAK of the VCM Transmissions was in stark contrast with the Transparency Server (TS) count PEAKING on the FIRST HOUR after voting closed. Unfortunately, all data from the TS have already been deleted that forced us to file a mandamus petition to the Supreme Court (SC) on November 3, 2022, for the SC to order the COMELEC and the Telcos to preserve and not alter their Transmission Logs involved in the 2022 Election.

On January 22, 2023, the SC ordered COMELEC, JCOC, CAC and the Telcos to comment on our petition to preserve the Transmission Logs. Before COMELEC has even submitted its comments to the SC, it published on March 23, 2023 in its website the List of VCM Received Transmissions Logs, which in reality are NOT Transmission Logs but Reception Logs.

It will be noticed that the Transmission Logs, proudly shown to the public on October 18, 2022 as a big improvement of the AES, is different from the Reception Logs shown to the public on March 23, 2023 in the COMELEC website. The Reception Logs was receiving data faster than the VCM transmissions specially in the FIRST TWO HOURS after voting closed at 7PM of May 9, 2022. It is quite obvious that the October 18, 2022 Graph was altered to "convince" the public that indeed there were 20M+ votes counted by the Transparency Server at 8:02PM of Election Day. First, the March 23, 2023 Graph PEAKED at the FIRST HOUR while the October 18, 2022 Graph PEAKED at the

SECOND HOUR as stated by Atty Laudiangco. Second, note that the FIRST HOUR Received Transmissions Rate of the March 23, 2023 Graph is much faster (631 VCMs per minute) than the VCM Transmissions Rate of October 18, 2022 (541 VCMs per minute).

That is why the deceptive Reception Logs was termed Received Transmission Logs to confuse us. We were asking for the VCM Transmission Logs, instead COMELEC had given us altered Reception Logs. This resulted in illogical data where VCM Transmission was received BEFORE that VCM had actually transmitted. An example of this is the transmission of the Malanday VCM which was received almost 3 minutes BEFORE the transmission was made. Also, still NOT answered by COMELEC to this very day was the discovery of NAMFREL that the Source Code may have been changed BEFORE downloaded to all VCMs.

Reflect on these events during this Holy Week. As the Christ was betrayed on the week of His Death, the Filipino People may have been betrayed last summer.

Comments

- **Jobo Elizes**
Comelec is trapped or caught with their pants down. This bungling by cheaters.

Edith Batalla
This message is only for those who know math and logic.

Mil Beb
Machines DON'T LIE, people especially from comelec DO!

Raul Eco
King sa kanta, "How can you stop the rain from falling down?" Kung sa batas, Let the documents speak for themselves." Comelec, your answer pls!

Dante San Juan Cambare
Congrats but no congrats comelec. You almost succeeded fooling us. Good n grateful that we have tntrio and the rest of the crusaders fighting for us

Audie Apayor
Concur po Sir!

Myk Sia
we know that this is the truth. but what are the chances that we will win this battle? how come the mainstream media are not picking this up?

oooooo

17
A CALL FOR PEACEFUL PUBLIC PROTEST
Ronnie Adriano Amoroso – April 2023

We, the undersigned UP Vanguards for Truth and Transparency, together with other individuals and organizations, call for peaceful, public protests in support of the impeachment of the Commissioners of the Commission on Elections and for the abolition of the Smartmatic partnership in future elections.

The COMELEC has failed the Filipino people and the Constitution by violating its mandate to protect the sanctity of the ballot by being the center of election irregularities and outright violations of the provisions of the Election Code.

1. It has allowed people with criminal records to run for public office, at many levels, forsaking its

mandate to ensure that candidates with good moral character occupy elective Government offices.

2. It surreptitiously printed tens of millions of ballots without independent supervision and observers in violation of procedures.

3. It changed the source codes of the voting machines and the allied electronic equipment without any supervision and without informing the independent observers.

4. It programmed and inserted the SIM cards that run the Vote Counting Machines (VCMs) without supervision and without foreknowledge of independent observers as to the programs and algorithms that went into the SIM cards.

5. It conducted a fraudulent count of the votes using the combination of the altered source codes and the insertion of the unaudited SIM cards.

As a result of the confluence of the above factors, and without thinking that knowledgeable and competent information technology professionals were watching every bit of information that was released by COMELEC, anomalous and highly irregular and improbable results were released to the public. In one instance, data released by none other than the COMELEC Chairman himself, contradicted the results from the reception logs that were provided by COMELEC.

Perhaps with the foreknowledge that the justice system would eventually acquit them, they violated with impunity a Supreme Court order to provide the Transmission Logs within a Court prescribed deadline. They still have not formally complied with the order to submit the Logs as of today.

We cannot allow a crooked COMELEC, NOW OR EVER, be the dictator of who will govern us, through their insidious machinations or through the Smartmatic machines banned even in its own country of origin. That is up to the Filipino voter who once trusted them to count our votes honestly and accurately.

We must make our voices heard now!
Ctto

oooooo

18

On April 3, 2023, COMELEC released a "Press Statement" through their Spokesperson Atty. John Rex Laudiangco "More Information on Uploading Total Transmission Logs to COMELEC Website" - Analysis by Eliseo Rio Jr – April 2023

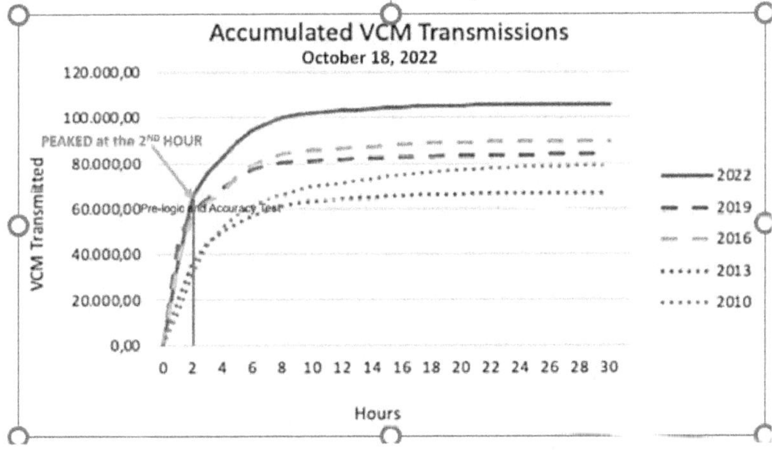

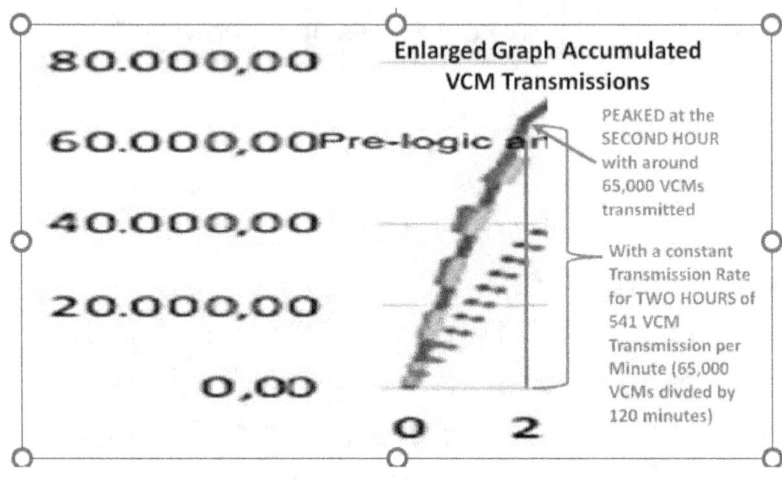

Enlarged Graph Accumulated VCM Transmissions
80.000,00
60.000,00 Pre-logic an
40.000,00
20.000,00
0,00
0
2
PEAKED at the SECOND HOUR with around 65,000 VCMs transmitted
With a constant Transmission Rate for TWO HOURS of 541 VCM Transmission per Minute (65,000 VCMs divded by 120 minutes)

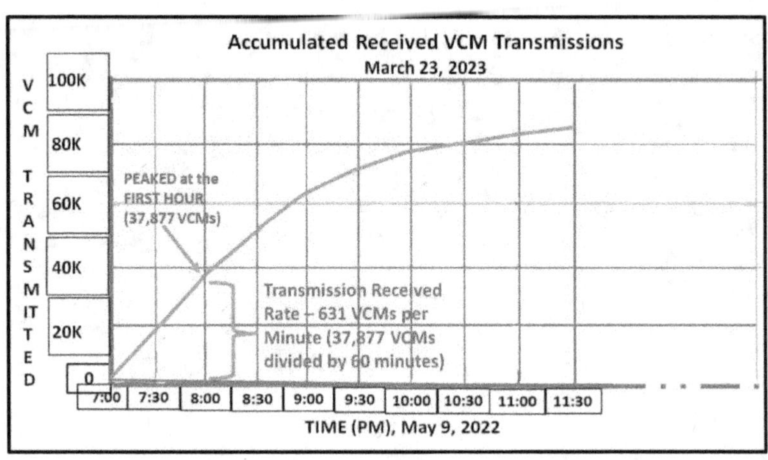

Accumulated Received VCM Transmissions
March 23, 2023
VCM TRANSMITTED
100K
80K
60K
40K
20K
0
PEAKED at the FIRST HOUR (37,877 VCMs)
Transmission Received Rate – 631 VCMs per Minute (37,877 VCMs divided by 60 minutes)
7:00 7:30 8:00 8:30 9:00 9:30 10:00 10:30 11:00 11:30
TIME (PM), May 9, 2022

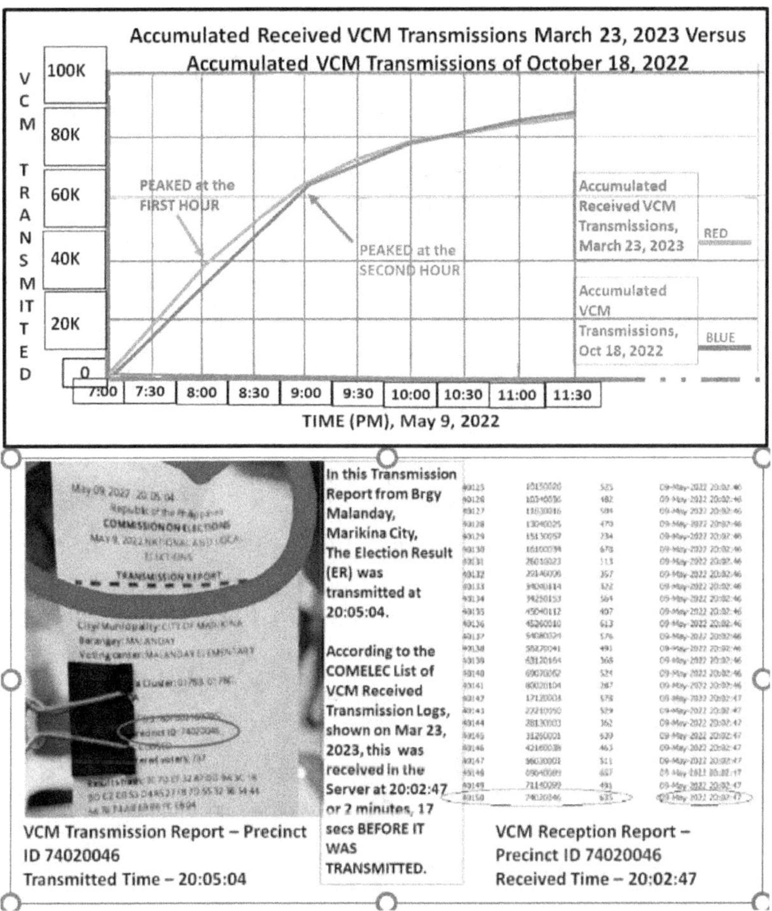

Noong Abril 3, 2023, nagpalabas ng "Press Statement" ang COMELEC sa pamamagitan ng kanilang Spokesperson na si Atty. John Rex Laudiangco "Ukol sa Karagdagang Impormasyon sa Pag-upload ng Kabuuang Transmission Logs sa COMELEC Website".

Inamin sa press statement na ito na "Mula sa naturang mga dokumento, ipinapakita ng Reception Date Time ang eksaktong punto at oras kung kailan natanggap ng Transparency Server ang Election Returns na mula sa mga Vote Counting Machines (VCMs)." Ngunit bakit "Reception Date Time" na galing sa Transparency Server ang ipinakitang mga dokumento na klarong sinabi ni COMELEC Chairman George Garcia na ipapakita ng COMELEC sa publiko ay ang

TRANSMISSION LOGS? Isa itong malaking panlilinlang sa publiko dahil ibang-iba ang TRANSMISSION LOGS SA RECEPTION LOGS! Ang napaka-kaduda-dudang resulta ng Transparency Server (TS) nga ang kinu-question, lalo na ang 20M+ na boto na ipinakita ng TS ng 8:02PM ng May 9, 2022, at ang imposibleng "constant vote ratio" na hindi nagbago sa kabuoan ng bilangan. At ito ang gustong palabasin ng COMELEC na TRANSMISSION LOGS?

Ang TRANSMISSION LOGS ay ang basehan ng ipinakita ng COMELEC sa publiko noong isang Forum na ginanap ng Oktubre 18, 2022, sa graph ng "Accumulated VCM Transmissions". Pinuri pa nga ni Atty Laudiangco ang bilis nito dahil nag-PEAK ang VCM transmissions ng PANGALAWANG ORAS. Ngunit ito ay taliwas sa resulta ng TS na ang bilang ng mga boto ay nag-PEAK sa UNANG ORAS. Bakit hindi itong TUNAY na TRANSMISSION LOGS na nag-PEAK ng pangalawang oras ang in-up-load sa Website? Bakit kailangang linlangin ang taumbayan na ang RECEPTION LOGS na galing sa TS na nag-PEAK ng unang oras ay ang ipinakitang "TRANSMISSION LOGS" kunwari?

Sinabi pa nga sa "Press Statement" na "Upang lalo pang mapatunayan ang integridad ng naturang Transmission Logs, ito ay maaaring i-corellate sa mga VCM logs na siyang magiging eksakto at 100% match sa nailathalang Reception Date Time."

Ito ay kasinungalingan! Iyung Transmission Date Time ng VCM ng Malanday Elementary School na may precinct ID 74020046 ay nag-transmit ng 20:05:04 habang sa Reception Date Time ng TS, ito ay na-receive ng 20:02:47. Anong himala ang nangyari na unang natanggap ng TS ang datos na hindi pa nai-transmit ng VCM sa humigit-kumulang na TATLONG MINUTO? Maraming ganitong halimbawa ang lalabas pa. Ito ang dahilan kung bakit ayaw ipakita ng COMELEC ang tunay na Transmission Logs: lalabas na mas mabilis ang bilang ng TS kaysa pag-transmit ng mga VCMs, at magpapakita na mayroon nagmanipula ng resulta ng TS.

Pinalabas din ng "Press Statement" na may mga election "watchdogs" na nagpakita na mataas ang accuracy ng pagbilang ng mga boto. Pero itong mga "watchdogs" ay walang kapangyarihan na mag-manman ng independente. Ang PPCRV ay binilang lang nang manual ang Election Results (ERs) ng bawat presinto na binigay sa kanila ng COMELEC. Mas mainam sana kung nai-kumpara nila ang mga ERs sa mga Vote Verified Paper Trail Audit (VVPAT) o resibo ng mga botante. Ang NAMFREL/LENTE naman ay hindi makapanumpa na hindi na-tamper ang mga balota na napili para sa Random Manual Audit (RMA), habang ang mga ito ay dinadala mula sa mga presinto hanggang sa Diamond Hotel, Maynila, dahil hindi naman nasubaybayan ng mga "watchdogs" ang prosesong ito. Walang kaibahan ito sa isang "magic trick" na magobserba ka lang, pero hindi mo pweding suriin ang patago na ginagawa ng "magician".

Kahit anong sabihin ng mga "election watchdogs" ay walang halaga ang mga ito kapag ayaw sagutin ng COMELEC ang mga simpleng tanong na ito:

1. Bakit hindi maipakita ng COMELEC ang tunay na Transmission Logs, iyung pinakita noong Oktubre 18, 2022, na ipinagmalaki pa nga ni Atty Laudiangco na nag-PEAK sa pangalawang oras?

2. Bakit nililinlang ng COMELEC ang publiko na sabihin na ang ipapakita nila ay Transmission Logs, ngunit mga Reception Logs pala ito?

3. Bakit ayaw sagutin ng COMELEC ang NAMFREL sa pagka-diskubre nila sa pagpalit ng source code na dinownload sa mga VCMs bago ng halalan?

4. Bakit magkaiba ang graph ng Reception Logs na binigay noon Marso 23, 2023, sa graph na pinakita ng COMELEC noon Oktubre 18, 2022?

5. Maipapakita ba ng COMELEC na kayang gawin ng Electoral Board (EB) ng mga presinto ang

lahat ng 9 tasks, lalo na ang pagimprenta ng walong (😎 kopya ng Election Results ng presinto, sa loob ng walong (😎 minuto lang (OTSO-OTSO)?

(English Translation)

On April 3, 2023, COMELEC released a "Press Statement" through their Spokesperson Atty. John Rex Laudiangco "More Information on Uploading Total Transmission Logs to COMELEC Website".

This press statement admitted that "From such documents, Reception Date Time shows the exact point and time when the Transparency Server received Election Returns from Vote Counting Machines (VCMs). " But why the "Reception Date Time" from Transparency Server showed documents that COMELEC Chairman George Garcia clearly stated that the COMELEC will show to the public are TRANSMISSION LOGS? This is a big scam to the public because TRANSMISSION LOGS are different from RECEPTION LOGS! The very questionable result of Transparency Server (TS) is being questioned, especially the 20M+ votes shown by TS at 8:02PM on May 9, 2022, and the impossible "constant vote ratio" that remained unchanged throughout the count. And this is what COMELEC wants to release TRANSMISSION LOGS?

TRANSMISSION LOGS is the basis of what COMELEC presented to the public during a Forum held on October 18, 2022, in the graph of "Accumulated VCM Transmissions". Atty Laudiangco even praised its speed because VCM transmissions PEAKED for the SECOND TIME. But this is contrary to TS results that the number of votes PEAKED IN THE FIRST TIME. Why are these not REAL TRANSMISSION LOGS that PEAKED for a second hour uploaded to the Website? Why do people need to be deceived that the RECEPTION LOGS from TS that PEAKED the first hour are the "TRANSMISSION LOGS" pretensely displayed?

It was said in the "Press Statement" that "To further prove the integrity of such Transmission Logs, it can be correlated with VCM logs that will be exactly and 100% match with the published Reception Date Time. "

This is a lie! The Transmission Date Time of VCM of Malanday Elementary School with precinct ID 74020046 transmitted at 20:05:04 while at the Reception Date Time of TS, it was received at 20:02:47. What miracle happened that TS first received data that VCM had not transmitted in approximately THREE MINUTES? Many of these examples will come out. This is why COMELEC doesn't want to show the real Transmission Logs: it will appear that TS count is faster than transmitting VCMs, and will show that someone manipulated TS results.

The "Press Statement" also released that there are election "watchdogs" that showed that the vote counting is high accuracy. But these "watchdogs" don't have the power to move independently. PPCRV just manually counted the Election Results (ERs) of each precinct given to them by the COMELEC. It would have been better if they had compared ERs to Vote Verified Paper Trail Audit (VVPAT) or voter receipts. NAMFREL/LENTE can't swear that the ballots selected for Random Manual Audit (RMA) were not tampered, while they were brought from the precincts to Diamond Hotel, Manila, because the "watchdogs" were not able to track this process. It's no different from a "magic trick" that you just observe, but you can't examine the hidden work of the "magician".

Whatever the "election watchdogs" say means nothing if COMELEC refuses to answer these simple questions:

1. Why can't COMELEC show the real Transmission Logs, the one you showed on October 18, 2022, that Atty Laudiangco is proud to PEAK in the second hour?

2. Why is COMELEC deceiving the public to say that what they will display is Transmission Logs, but they are Reception Logs?

3. Why is COMELEC not responding to NAMFREL on their discovery of changing the source code downloaded on VCMs prior to the election?

4. Why is the graph of Reception Logs given before March 23, 2023, different from the graph shown by COMELEC on October 18, 2022?

5. Can the COMELEC show that the Electoral Board (EB) of the precincts can do all 9 tasks, especially printing eight (😎 copies of the precinct Election Results, in just eight (😎 minutes (OTSO)?

ooooooo

19
Here's NGOs and assns Manifesto which parallels People's Mandamus and TNTrio' s SC mandamus: - Franklin Ysaac – April 2023

Inviting only groups to sign this Manifesto but they should not be affiliated with any political party .

M A N I F E S T O

"Whereas the people have spoken in various media outlets and Supreme Court petition questioning the non release of true and legit transmission logs in the May 2022 election .

"Whereas, we are invoking the Freedom of Information Act and Constitutional Right to Know the Truth,

"Therefore, we, members of NGO and private groups and associations who are advocates of truth, transparency and good governance, hereby express our full support to SC mandamus petition by TNTrio, the People's On line Mandamus compelling the Comission of Election to release the true and legit transmission logs to erase any doubt about the last election and to ensure and secure that the future elections will not be compromised again by non release of authentic and verified transmission logs to the people ."

Signed

NGOs and private groups/ associations .

Please take note this will be published in major dailies both in social and print media .

oooooo

20
Comelec Official Cheated
Big-Time -
Mar Tecson – April 2023

If it is quite clear that Comelec officials cheated big-time in the last election, and then they refuse to do their obligation to release the needed data or devices being repeatedly asked by petitioners before them and the Supreme Court, can sympathizers of the petitioning retired military officials make a citizen arrest of the Comelec officials— in order to force the issue against them?

oooooo

21

Holy Week Reflections: Why did God become human in Jesus? – Tina A. Astorga – April 2023

HOLY WEEK REFLECTIONS: Why did God become human in Jesus? Why did Jesus die on the cross? What is the meaning of the Resurrection?

We were taught that Jesus had to die in our place for our sins to appease God's anger whose majesty was violated. This is wrong theology. This shows a vengeful God whose anger must be appeased before he forgives; a vengeful God who sent his own son to die in our place for the sins that violated his divine majesty. Who is a father who does this to his son?

What does good and correct theology teaches us? God has loved us even while we are sinners. And it is because of God's unconditional love that touches us at our core, at our very depths, that we seek to renew our lives. In the end, only love---unconditional love, that can change us. Jesus taught us about a love like this in the story of the prodigal son.

The more primary question is why did God become human in Jesus? Because God is love, and it is the very nature of love to seek total union with the beloved. Thus, there is no pain, suffering, sorrow that is ours which is not Jesus's, and so also are our joys! Jesus became like us in everything, except sin.

But why did he die on the cross? It is because he came into a world of sin, where the reign of God which he preached came into collision with the powers of his time. He preached the reign of God, where there was justice for all, particularly for the poor and marginalized, where the sick and the leper were cared for, where women were honored and valued, where the despised and the downtrodden were embraced with compassion.

He died, because of the way he lived-- fighting for truth and justice, calling us to do the same in our own time. To be a Christian, thus, is to become more and more like Jesus we love, by living a life of truth, in our fight for justice.

Because of the way Jesus lived, and the way he died, light overcame darkness, life conquered death, and love crushed sin. The Resurrection of Jesus is where our radical hope lies. No matter what a mess we make of our lives, and the same of this world, the FINAL WORD is not darkness but light, not death but life, not sin but love.

This is our Easter hope on which our whole life is based.

oooooo

22
HERE IS INDISPUTABLE PROOF THAT PRINTING 8 COPIES OF THE PRECINCT ELECTION RESULT (ER) TAKES NO LESS THAN 12 MINUTES. - Eliseo Rio Jr – April 2023

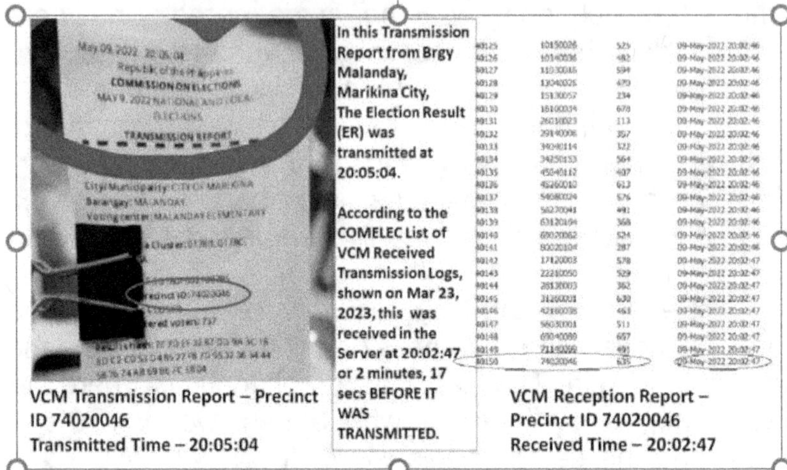

In this Transmission Report from Brgy Malanday, Marikina City, The Election Result (ER) was transmitted at 20:05:04.

According to the COMELEC List of VCM Received Transmission Logs, shown on Mar 23, 2023, this was received in the Server at 20:02:47 or 2 minutes, 17 secs BEFORE IT WAS TRANSMITTED.

VCM Transmission Report – Precinct ID 74020046
Transmitted Time – 20:05:04

VCM Reception Report – Precinct ID 74020046
Received Time – 20:02:47

COMELEC General Instructions Resolution 10762
Promulgated on 16 February 2022 for the 9 May 2022 Elections

Part VII = Tasks for Closing the Voting Period

Summaries of Tasks "A" to "F":

A. Authentication Procedure for Electoral Board Chairperson.
B. Authentication Procedure for Electoral Board Clerk and 3rd Member.
C. Touch "Close Voting" in the Vote Counting Machine Touch Screen.
D. Input Personal Identification Number of Clerk.
E. Input Personal Identification Number of 3rd Member.
F. Embed "Role Personal Identification Number" to the Election Result.

Task "G": The Vote Counting Machine shall print the eight (8) copies of the Election Returns. Detach the Election Returns and place them in the envelopes provided for the purpose.

Tasks "H" and "I" = Procedures for preparation of the Global System for Mobile (GSM) communications device = either DITO Tele Community or Globe Telecom or Smart Communications = for electronic transmission.

HERE IS INDISPUTABLE PROOF THAT PRINTING 8 COPIES OF THE PRECINCT ELECTION RESULT (ER) TAKES NO LESS THAN 12 MINUTES.

Of the 9 Major tasks required by COMELEC General Instructions to be done BEFORE the Precinct's Election Result (ER) can be transmitted by the VCM, the longest task is the printing of 8 copies of the ER. The two video clips below show that printing 1 copy of the National ER takes 1 minute or 8 minutes for the 8 copies. The printing of 1 copy of the Local ER takes 30 seconds or 4 minutes for the 8 copies. Printing 8 copies of the National and Local ERs will take at least 12 minutes.

There are 9 major tasks required by the COMELEC General Instructions to be accomplished BEFORE the precinct's Election Result (ER) can be transmitted to the Transparency Server (TS). The longest of these 9 tasks is the printing of 8 copies of the ER.

From the COMELEC Hands-On Lecture Demo Video of VCM operations for the 2022 Election, these 9 Major tasks have to be done sequentially as the VCM won't go to the next task without finishing a previous task. The total time from closing the precinct voting to actual transmissions will be impossible to attain in 8 minutes as printing the 8 copies of ERs takes already 12 minutes! The total time for completing the 9 Major tasks will be around 19 minutes. The earliest time of transmissions therefore would be 7:19PM NOT 7:08PM of May 9, 2022. Closing the voting BEFORE 7:00PM is illegal because it may disenfranchise a voter who arrives a minute before the official closing time of 7PM. Also, it is incredible that the VCMs were able to transmit 20M+ votes from 7:19PM to 8PM, yet between 8PM to 9PM, a whole hour, the votes transmitted unexpectedly dropped to just 13.2M+ votes.

We have challenged COMELEC to demonstrate to the public that it is possible to finish all 9 major tasks after closing the voting to transmitting the ERs in just 8 minutes. We demand an answer from COMELEC to explain why 5,552 VCMs transmissions were received in the Transparency Server BEFORE the VCM transmissions started at 7:19 PM, as shown in the Reception Logs uploaded in their website. A clear example of the Server receiving data AHEAD of the VCM transmission is the one from Malanday Elementary School at Marikina City where the 19:05:04 transmission time was received at 19:02:47 in the server. We demand that COMELEC show the REAL Transmission Logs, verified through the Call Details Records (CDR) of the Telcos involved in the transmission of data from the VCMs to the Transparency Server. We demand that COMELEC explain the discovery of NAMFREL that the VCM Source Code may have been altered BEFORE the 2022 Election.

IT IS OUR RIGHT AS REGISTERED VOTERS TO MAKE SURE THAT THE 2022 ELECTION WAS NOT RIGGED!

oooooo

23
Supplemental Petition to compel Comelec to release true and legIt transmission logs - Franklin Ysaac – April 2023

To all followers,

Our supplemental petition to compel Comelec to release true and legit transmission logs and not reception logs has been acknowledged received by the Supreme Court .

For your info.

TO ALL WHOM THIS MAY CONCERN:

We hereby acknowledge the receipt of your email (THIS THREAD) in accordance with the **Revised Guidelines on Submission of Electronic Copies of Supreme Court-Bound Paper** pursuant to *A.M. No. 10-3-7-SC (Re: Proposed Rules on E-Filing) and A.M. No. 11-9-4-SC (Re: Proposed Rule for the Efficient Use of Paper).*

For your information and guidance.

Respectfully,

JUDICIAL RECORDS OFFICE (E-Filing)
*Ground Floor, New Supreme Court Building
Supreme Court of the Philippines
Padre Faura Street, Ermita, Manila   1000*
☎ *8523-6464*

Note: As of May 31, 2022, the Supreme Court has approved the Revised Guidelines on Submission of Electronic Copies of SC-Bound Papers.
For more info please click on the link below:

https://sc.judiciary.gov.ph/27487/

oooooo

24
A CALL FOR PEACEFUL PUBLIC PROTEST –
Quo vadis, Filipinas ? –
April 2023

OUR REAL PRESIDENT LENI ROBREDO 🇵🇭
Quo vadis, Filipinas ? · ·

A CALL FOR PEACEFUL PUBLIC PROTEST

We, the undersigned UP Vanguards for Truth and Transparency, together with other individuals and organizations, call for peaceful, public protests in support of the impeachment of the Commissioners of the Commission on Elections and for the abolition of the Smartmatic partnership in future elections.

The COMELEC has failed the Filipino people and the Constitution by violating its mandate to protect the sanctity of the ballot by being the center of election irregularities and outright violations of the provisions of the Election Code.

1. It has allowed people with criminal records to run for public office, at many levels, forsaking its mandate to ensure that candidates with good moral character occupy elective Government offices.

2. It surreptitiously printed tens of millions of ballots without independent supervision and observers in violation of procedures.

3. It changed the source codes of the voting machines and the allied electronic equipment without any supervision and without informing the independent observers.

4. It programmed and inserted the SIM cards that run the Vote Counting Machines (VCMs) without supervision and without foreknowledge of independent observers as to the programs and algorithms that went into the SIM cards.

5. It conducted a fraudulent count of the votes using the combination of the altered source codes and the insertion of the unaudited SIM cards.

As a result of the confluence of the above factors, and without thinking that knowledgeable and competent information technology professionals were watching every bit of information that was released by COMELEC, anomalous and highly irregular and improbable results were released to the public. In one instance, data released by none other than the COMELEC Chairman himself, contradicted the results from the reception logs that were provided by COMELEC.

Perhaps with the foreknowledge that the justice system would eventually acquit them, they violated with impunity a Supreme Court order to provide the Transmission Logs within a Court prescribed deadline. They still have not formally complied with the order to submit the Logs as of today.

We cannot allow a crooked COMELEC, NOW OR EVER, be the dictator of who will govern us, through their insidious machinations or through the Smartmatic machines banned even in its own country of origin. That is up to the Filipino voter who once trusted them to count our votes honestly and accurately.

We must make our voices heard now!
Ctto

AFP PNP WILL PROTECT THE PEOPLE AND CONSTITUTION!
IMPEACH COMELEC! PEOPLE POWER

oooooo

25
Source Code in all VCM's changed – Elisep Rio Jr. – April 2023

Eliseo Rio Jr

Yesterday at 8:39 PM · 🌐

•••

Namfrel discovered that the Source Code in all VCMs may have been changed from the Source Code that had undergone review. COMELEC initially brushed this off as just a "typo error", but NAMFREL insisted on a Source Code Review of the program already downloaded in ALL VCMs before the 2022 Election. COMELEC said that this will cause delays and the review can be made after Election Day. COMELEC never did.

oooooo

26
Comelec is a Duterte-Marcos Body – Tina A. Astorga – April 2023

OUR REAL PRESIDENT LENI ROBREDO 🇵🇭
Quo vadis, Filipinas ?
COMELEC IS A DUTERTE-MARCOS BODY WITH DENNIS UY, DUTERTE'S CRONY AS THE HANDLER OF ALL ELECTION MATERIALS.

George Garcia (Chair) Ex-Marcos Lawyer
Commissioners
1. Aimee Ferolino (Davao)
2. Socorro Inting (Davao)
3. Aimee Neri (Davao)
4. Rey Bulay (Duterte's frat brother)
5. Saidamen Pangarungan (Duterte's classmate)
6. Marlon Casquejo (Davao)
Dennis Uy (F2 Logistics)- Duterte crony

In-charge of transporting ballots, voting machines, SD cards, election returns from Comelec to designated precincts before election day.

Imee Marcos: Senate Elections Reforms Chairperson
Tina A. Astorga

oooooo

27

REQUEST IN PURSUIT OF ELECTION TRUTH – Ronnie Adrianos Amoroso – April 2023

Reference Supreme Court Resolution dated January 10, 2023

Case No. G.R. 263838 Mandamus Petition by the TNTrio

President and CEO
TELCO - GLOBE TELECOM
TELCO - SMART COMMUNICATIONS
TELCO - DITO TELECOMMUNITY
Dear Sir:

Please be advised that I am but one of the multi-millions of subscribers/customers of your TELCO. If I may humbly add, I am a concerned senior citizen, tax payer, registered voter, and patriot.

Whereas, the Philippines 1987 Constitution/Saligang Batas (Section 28, Article II and Section 7, Article III) have vested in me and in us, Philippinos, the FOI (Freedom of Information);

Whereas, the Executive Order No. 02, s. 2016 has urgently operationalized the said Constitutional provisions and has vested in me and in us, Philippinos, the FOI (Freedom of Information);

Whereas, the Data Privacy Act of 2012 (R.A. 10173) and your Non-Disclosure Policy are INFERIOR and SERVANT to the 1987 Constitution/Saligang Batas and to the Executive Order No. 02, s. 2016;

Now, therefore, I, by virtue of the powers vested in me by the Constitution and by the Executive Order No. 02, s. 2016, do hereby request/demand urgently from you, TELCO, the following:

1. Full Disclosure of TELCO Call Detail Records (CDR) from each and every VCM that transmitted data through your network for the national election exercise on May 9, 2022 from 7.01 evening to 9.00 evening.

2. In addition to the complete CDR, Full Disclosure of all records including account name, clustered precinct number, location, MSISDN (mobile number), time of connection start, time of connection end, size of data transmitted, etc., location of the mobile tower that each VCM connected to and the IP addresses to which the data transmissions were sent.

Kindly oblige to reply and satisfy my humble demand/request at your earliest, within five (5) days from date hereof, suffice to state that should likewise comply to the Supreme Court Resolution dated January 10, 2023, Case No. G.R. 263838 Mandamus Petition by the TNTrio

With all due respect,

oooooo

28
Comelec Deletes Backup Files Used in May 9, 2022 Polls – Francisco S. Tatad, Inquirer.net – posted at fb by Rochelle Santos – April 12, 2023

Never forget

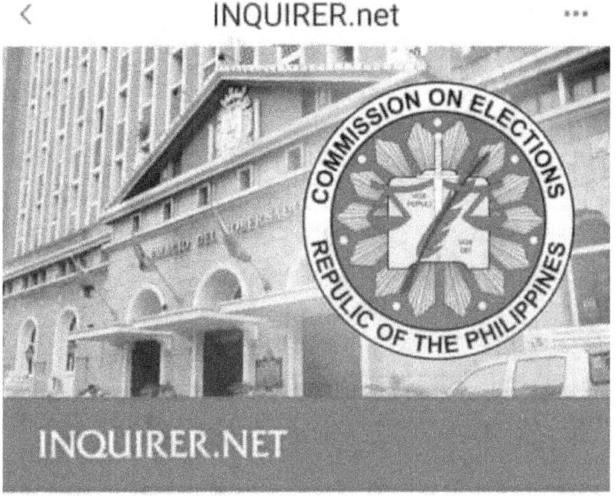

FIRST THINGS FIRST
By Francisco S. Tatad

A retired military officer's threat to impeach the chairman and four other commissioners of the Commission on Elections has led to a comedy of errors involving the Comelec, a three–man post–election transparency team and a sizeable group of former high-ranking military officers.

Unlike any other comedy, no one is laughing. Invoking his constitutional right as a citizen, retired Col. Leonardo O. Odoño, a member of Philippine Military Academy Class of 1964, threatened action against the Comelec commissioners if they failed to validate certain data related to the first-hour vote count after the voting ended at 7PM on May 9, 2022.

Odoño was expressing full support for a petition filed by retired general and former undersecretary of the Department of Information and Communication Technology (DICT) Eliseo Rio, former Namfrel chairman Augusto Lagman, and former president of the Financial Executives Institute of the Philippines (Finex) Franklin Ysaac, seeking the release of the voting transmission logs during that first hour.

The Eliseo Rio group believes the over 20 million vote count is "statistically improbable" and can be validated only by cross-checking it with the officially stamped and signed transmission logs from the vote-counting machines (VCMs). But the Comelec has completely ignored the petition since last October. It was only after Odoño camo into the picture and threatened action against the Comelec commissioners that things started moving.

Under the Constitution, any citizen upon a resolution of endorsement by a member of Congress may file a verified complaint of impeachment against the president, the vice president, members of the Supreme Court, members of the constitutional commissions, and the Ombudsman for culpable violation of the Constitution, treason, bribery, graft and corruption, other high crimes, or betrayal of public trust.

Two former AFP chiefs of staff and nearly a hundred "cavaliers" (PMA graduates) issued a manifesto expressing solidarity with Odoño and a desire to be identified with the impeachment complaint. These are Gen. Alexander Yano, Class '76, who served as AFP chief of staff under President Gloria Macapagal Arroyo (and later as ambassador to Brunei), and Gen. Jessie Dellusa, Class '79, who served under President Noynoy Aquino. The list includes cavaliers from various PMA classes, from '57 up.

No one in the Rio group nor in the cavaliers group is related to any anti-government political faction. Rio himself began his career as a Marcos scientist under Executive Secretary Alejandro Melchor during the Maphilindo days when the Philippines and Indonesia were openly at odds with Malaysia. He worked on the Santa Barbara national security project that tried to develop the first Philippine indigenous missile. He was sent by Marcos to study advanced missile technology in Germany and India. As DICT undersecretary under President Rodrigo Duterte, he provided the organization its initial direction before it was taken over by its first secretary, former senator Gregorio Honasan, and its current head, Secretary Ivan Uy.

The group's interest was provoked by the over 20 million transmission rate at the first hour after the voting, and then its drastic drop to 13.2 million during the second hour. At this first hour, Comelec General Instructions Resolution 10762 requires every precinct electoral board (EB) to perform nine major tasks before it can begin transmitting the election returns (ERs). The longest of these tasks is the printing of eight copies of the ERs per precinct. Time and motion studies have shown that all these tasks could not be accomplished in less than half an hour.

This means that transmission at the first hour could only begin after 7:30PM or so, not earlier. Which further means that if the precincts could transmit over 20 million votes at the first hour, after accomplishing the nine major tasks, then they should have been able to transmit twice that number, at the second hour. But it was able to transmit 13.2 million votes in only one full hour. This means it could not have transmitted over 20 million votes in the first half-hour.

Faced with the prospect of a significant portion of the military endorsing an impeachment suit against its commissioners, the Comelec announced the release, through its website, of the "transmission logs" the Rio group had been requesting since last October. This was received with great relief. But upon cursory examination of the data, the Eliseo Rio group saw that what the Comelec had sent them were the "reception logs from the transparency servers," rather than the "transmission logs from the VCMs." One is not the same as the other, and it is not clear whether the Comelec committed an honest mistake or has decided to engage in duplicity or double-dealing. Pending a final word from Eliseo Rio's group and the cavaliers, we cannot say how long we'll get stuck with this can of worms.

oooooo

29
Request to Smartmatic Company – by a private citizen – Ronnie Adriano Amoroso -

1:42   🔋 ⬛⬛⬛ ⠿ ◎ ・   📶 53%🔋

←   Fwd: REQUEST IN PURSUIT ...

REQUEST IN PURSUIT OF ELECTION
TRUTH,
Reference Supreme Court Resolution
dated January 10, 2023
Case No. G.R. 263838 Mandamus
Petition by the TNTrio

Mr. Alfredo S. Panlilio
President and CEO and CRO - Smart
Communications
Email: apanlilio@smart.com.ph

Dear Sir:

Please be advised that I am but one of the
multi-millions of subscribers/customers
of Smart Communications. If I may
humbly add, I am a concerned senior
citizen, tax payer, registered voter, and
patriot.

Whereas, the Philippines 1987
Constitution/Saligang Batas (Section 28,
Article II and Section 7, Article III) have
vested in me and in us, Philippinos, the
FOI (Freedom of Information);

Whereas, the Executive Order No. 02. s.

🗑   📭   📤   ↩   ⋮
Delete   Archive   Move   Reply all   More

||| ◯   ‹

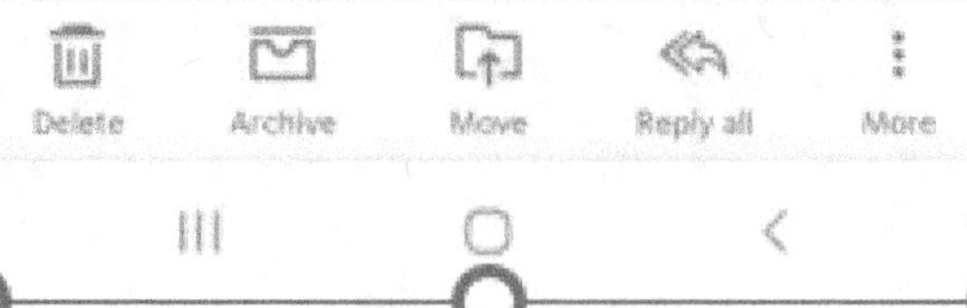

←   Fwd: REQUEST IN PURSUIT ...

Whereas, the Executive Order No. 02, s. 2016 has urgently operationalized the said Constitutional provisions and has vested in me and in us, Philippinos, the FOI (Freedom of Information);

Whereas, the Data Privacy Act of 2012 (R.A. 10173) and your Non-Disclosure Policy are INFERIOR and SERVANT to the 1987 Constitution/Saligang Batas and to the Executive Order No. 02, s. 2016;

Now, therefore, I, by virtue of the powers vested in me by the Constitution and by the Executive Order No. 02, s. 2016, do hereby request/demand urgently from you, Smart Communications, the following:

1. Full Disclosure of Smart Communications Call Detail Records (CDR) from each and every VCM that transmitted data through your network for the national election exercise on May 9, 2022 from 7.01 evening to 9.00 evening.

2. In addition to the complete CDR, Full Disclosure of all records including account name, clustered precinct number

←   Fwd: REQUEST IN PURSUIT …

2. In addition to the complete CDR, Full Disclosure of all records including account name, clustered precinct number location, MSISDN (mobile number), time of connection start, time of connection end, size of data transmitted, etc., location of the mobile tower that each VCM connected to and the IP addresses to which the data transmissions were sent.

Kindly oblige to reply and satisfy my humble demand/request at your earliest, within five (5) days from date hereof, suffice to state that should likewise comply to the Supreme Court Resolution dated January 10, 2023, Case No. G.R. 263838 Mandamus Petition by the TNTrio.

With all due respect,
Ronnie Adriano R. Amoroso
Subscriber/Customer, Concerned senior citizen, Tax payer, Registered voter, and Patriot.
Concepcion Grande, Naga City 4400,
Camarines Sur, Bicol Region

Republic of the Philippines
Supreme Court
Baguio City

EN BANC

NOTICE

Sirs/Mesdames:

Please take notice that the Court en banc issued a Resolution dated **JANUARY 10, 2023,** *which reads as follows:*

"**G.R. No. 263838** (Eliseo Mijares Rio, Jr., Augusto Cadeliña Lagman and Franklin Fayloga Ysaac vs. Commission on Elections, Smartmatic Total Information Management, DITO Telecommunity, Globe Telecom, and Smart Communications).- The Court Resolved to **IMPLEAD** the Joint Congressional Oversight Committee on Automated Election System (JCOC) and the Commission on Elections (COMELEC) Advisory Council (CAC) as respondents.

Acting on the 'Petition for Mandamus with Prayer for Temporary Restraining Order (TRO) to Compel Preservation and/or Restrain Alteration/Erasure/Deletion of Subscriber and Cyber Traffic Data Integrity of Telecom Transmissions of National Election Results from 7pm to at Least 9pm of May 9, 2022 Philippines Time,' the Court Resolved, without giving due course to the petition, to

(a) **REQUIRE** respondents COMELEC, JCOC and CAC to **COMMENT** on the petition and prayer for TRO and/or injunction within ten (10) days from notice hereof; and

(b) **REQUIRE** the petitioners to **COMPLY**, within five (5) days from notice hereof, with the following procedural requirements:

(i) requirement to submit proper verification pursuant to Section 5, Rule 64, in relation to Section 4, Rule 7, 1997 Rules of Civil Procedure, as amended, it appearing that the attestations in the verification are incomplete;

(ii) requirement to submit proper proof of service (*e.g.*, a written admission of the party served, or an affidavit of the party serving and registry receipts) of the petition on the adverse parties pursuant to Section 5, Rule 64 in relation to Section 17, Rule 13, same Rules, it appearing

*SMARTMATIC TOTAL INFORMATION MANAGEMENT (reg)
Unit 2208, 22F The Trade and Financial Tower
7th Avenue corner 32nd Street
Bonifacio Global City, 1634 Taguig

*ERNESTO R. ALBERTO (reg)
DITO CME Holdings President
DITO Tele Community
21st Floor UDENNA Tower
Rizal Driver corner 4th Avenue
Bonifacio Global City, 1634 Taguig

*ERNEST L. CU (reg)
Globe Telecom President
Globe Tower @ 2nd Street corner 7th Avenue
Bonifacio Global City, 1634 Taguig

*ALFREDO S. PANLILIO (reg)
Smart Communications President
Ramon Cojuangco Building
Makati Avenue corner Ayala Avenue
Legaspi Village, Makati City

**THE SOLICITOR GENERAL (reg)

Notice of Resolution   - 2 -   G.R. No. 263838
January 10, 2023

that the Affidavit of Service was notarized before the actual date of posting of the copy of the petition; and

(iii) requirement to submit (i) an electronic copy of the petition and its annexes and (ii) a verified declaration that the electronic copy is a complete and true copy of the printed document and annexes filed with the Court, as required in the Guidelines on Submission and Processing of Soft Copies of Supreme Court-bound Papers Pursuant to the Efficient Use of Paper Rule.

The Court further Resolved to **NOTE** the

(a) Electronic Email dated November 7, 2022 of Ronnie Adriano R. Amoroso, Concerned Citizen Taxpayer, Registered Voter, Concepcion Grande, 4400 Naga City, requesting the Court to issue a TRO; and

(b) Electronic Email dated November 16, 2022 of Gregorio T. Mariano, Jr., M.D., stating, among others, that he is intervening in support of this case." Hernando, J., on leave. (65)

By authority of the Court:

MARIFE M. LOMIBAO-CUEVAS
Clerk of Court Sr.

TO ALL WHOM THIS MAY CONCERN:

We hereby acknowledge the receipt of your email (THIS THREAD) in accordance with the **Revised Guidelines on Submission of Electronic Copies of Supreme Court-Bound Paper** pursuant to *A.M. No. 10-3-7-SC (Re: Proposed Rules on E-Filing) and A.M. No. 11-9-4-SC (Re: Proposed Rule for the Efficient Use of Paper).*

For your information and guidance.

Respectfully,

JUDICIAL RECORDS OFFICE (E-Filing)

Ground Floor, New Supreme Court Building
Supreme Court of the Philippines
Padre Faura Street, Ermita, Manila   1000
☎ *8523-6464*

Note: As of May 31, 2022, the Supreme Court has approved the Revised Guidelines on Submission of Electronic Copies of SC-Bound Papers.
For more info please click on the link below:

https://sc.judiciary.gov.ph/27487/

ooooooo

30
A new Petition via Change.org – Mandamus toCompel Comelec to disclose the True Transmission Logs

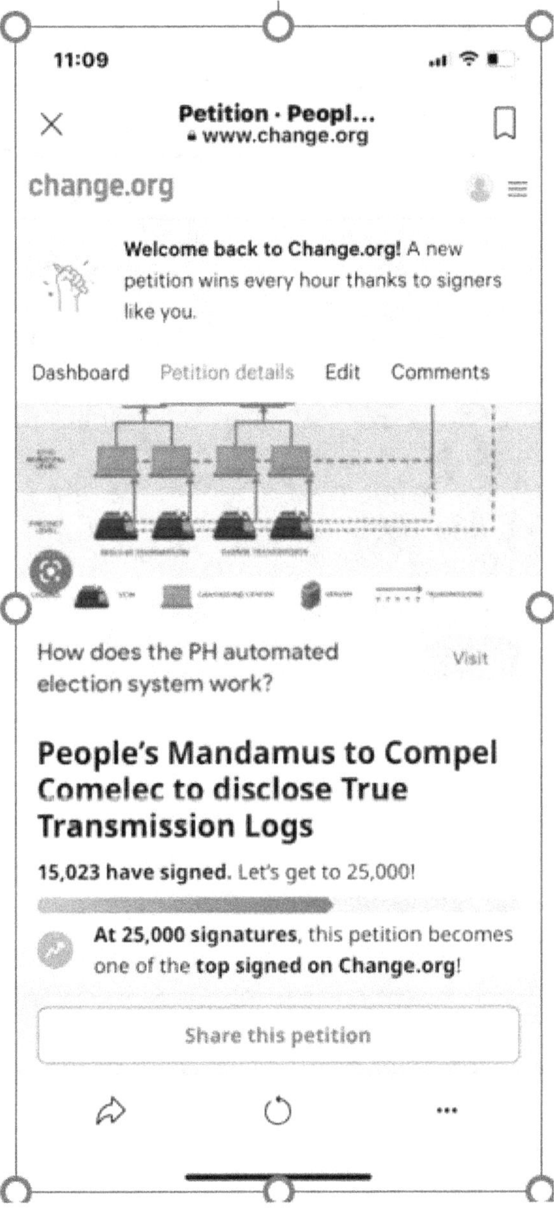

oooooo

31

A CALL FOR PEACEFUL PUBLIC PROTEST –
Eliseo Rio Jr – April 2023

.A CALL FOR PEACEFUL PUBLIC PROTEST

We, the undersigned UP Vanguards for Truth and Transparency, together with other individuals and organizations, call for peaceful, public protests in support of the impeachment of the Commissioners of the Commission on Elections and for the abolition of the Smartmatic partnership in future elections.

The COMELEC has failed the Filipino people and the Constitution by violating its mandate to protect the sanctity of the ballot by being the center of election irregularities and outright violations of the provisions of the Election Code.

1. It has allowed people with criminal records to run for public office, at many levels, forsaking its mandate to ensure that candidates with good moral character occupy elective Government offices.

2. It surreptitiously printed tens of millions of ballots without independent supervision and observers in violation of procedures.

3. It changed the source codes of the voting machines and the allied electronic equipment without any supervision and without informing the independent observers.

4. It programmed and inserted the SIM cards that run the Vote Counting Machines (VCMs) without supervision and without foreknowledge of independent observers as to the programs and algorithms that went into the SIM cards.

5. It conducted a fraudulent count of the votes using the combination of the altered source codes and the insertion of the unaudited SIM cards.

As a result of the confluence of the above factors, and without thinking that knowledgeable and competent information technology professionals were watching every bit of information that was released by COMELEC, anomalous and highly irregular and improbable results were released to the public. In one instance, data released by none other than the COMELEC Chairman himself, contradicted the results from the reception logs that were provided by COMELEC.

Perhaps with the foreknowledge that the justice system would eventually acquit them, they violated with impunity a Supreme Court order to provide the Transmission Logs within a Court prescribed deadline. They still have not formally complied with the order to submit the Logs as of today.

We cannot allow a crooked COMELEC, NOW OR EVER, be the dictator of who will govern us, through their insidious machinations or through the Smartmatic machines banned even in its own country of origin. That is up to the Filipino voter who once trusted them to count our votes honestly and accurately.

We must make our voices heard now!
1. Ephraim Rio '69
2. Eliseo Rio Jr. '65
3. Max Montenegro '72
4. Alben B. Manuel '94
5. Edwin V. Fernandez '70
6. Timothy Elbert Tan '83
7. Pons Carpio' 81
8. Bill Pamintuan '83
9. Gari Garcia 67
10. Ben de Leon '57
11. Bong Flores '83
12. Marvin Villamor Juan '88
13. Jimmy Rodriguez '86

14. Emy Rodriguez '86
15. Auggie Isberto '80
16. Rey Ascano '80
17. Ray Paolo Santiago '96
18. Cid Diomampo '71
19. Sean Luke Dado' 90
20. Jobert Po '98
21. Adrian Atas '11
22. Sancho Exevea '77
23. Albert Joseph Carreon '04
24. Maricel Agapito '95
25. Rodil De Los Reyes '88
26. Toots Tagle '94
27. Diego M. Panganiban '69
28. Vic Sevilla '73
29. Malou Ocampo-Macrohon '87
30. Chino Wasan '99
31. Randy Dacanay '83
32. Pabs Villegas '69
33. Steven Reyes ''93
34. Volts Beltran '94
35. Niels Ian Badillo '06
36. Floro R. Francisco '80
37. Marc Rodriguera "95
38. Ruben Posadas '69
39. Jennie Ablog '20
40. Armando Dabandan '96
41. Paul Yapjoco '90
42. Dominador Victor M Catibog '89
43. Benito "BB" Bernardo '71
44. Gemma Rose Cayanan '18
45. Renold M Verano '05
46. Lito Legaspi '66
47. Gege Polvito '21
48. John Fortes '70
49. Vic Gomez '07
50. Joesa Lyn "Jai" Villaruel '18
51. Gigi Ariñas '12

52. Isidro Junior Aragon '78
53. Vida Dizon Vergel '80
54. Salvador Oblena '97
55. Ray Alindong '95
56. Dave Austria '70
57. Rene Villafuerte '90
58. Gil Abrazado '80
59. John Ma. R. Chumacera "86
60. Generoso R. Dimasuay '80
61. Raoul Buizon '80
62. Santi JOSON '80
63. Manny Reyes '80
64. Kenneth Tirado 99
65. Danilo G. Supnet '85
66. Mathew D Alcala '14
67. Nhell Dolot '80
68. Ronnie Cabrillos '05
69. Daniel Manuel O. Macrohon, Jr. '13
70. Frederic de Jesus '93
71. Marlea Muñez '88
72. Ian Alvaera '02
73. Patrick Provido Jr '02
74. Kholin Marie Decena-Provido '03
75. Eduardo Bolivar Jr. '03
76. Philip Michael de los Santos '02
77. Timie Cura-Biola '94
78. Mark Vergel Borja '14
79. Mickaella Manuud '19

Gari Sopena commented

Mark Santos - That is exactly what they're doing now. They're just waiting for comelec to submit the vcm transmission reports to compare it against the receptions logs and all the other data they have collected to see if they all match up. You don't just file a case without a strong evidence, do you? Ganun ka ba ka-tanga?

ooooo

32
More Delays coming - Franklin Ysaac – April 2023

Just received this email from SC clerk of court at 230PM today.

The request of Comelec for extension for 30 days already expired. But it may request for another extension according to our sources.

More delays coming.

Republic of the Philippines
Supreme Court
Manila

EN BANC

NOTICE

Sirs/Mesdames:

Please take notice that the Court en banc issued a Resolution dated **MARCH 8, 2023**, which reads as follows:

"G.R. No. 263838 (Eliseo Mijares Rio, Jr., et al. vs. Commission on Elections, et al.) – The Court Resolved to

(a) **NOTE** the Compliance (with the resolution dated January 10, 2023) and Manifestation dated February 24, 2023 filed by counsel for petitioners, submitting the original (i) Verification/Certification and (ii) Affidavit of Service; and stating that the electronic copy of the petition and its annexes were submitted via e-mail on November 4, 2022, receipt of which was acknowledged by the Court's Judicial Records Office;

(b) **NOTE** and **GRANT** the Notice of Withdrawal of Appearance dated February 24, 2023 filed by Atty. Kates Justin E. Aguilar, withdrawing her appearance as counsel for petitioners, with the latter's conformity; and requesting that all notices, resolutions and other processes of the Court, and all pleadings, motions and correspondence from the other parties be sent directly to the respective addresses of the petitioners and/or to any counsel who may subsequently enter his/her appearance on their behalf; and

(c) **GRANT** the Motion dated March 2, 2023 filed by the Office of the Solicitor General for the Commission on Elections (COMELEC) and the COMELEC Advisory Council for an extension of thirty (30) days from March 3, 2023, or until April 2, 2023, within which to file a comment on the petition." Dimaampao, J., on leave. (44 & 83)

By authority of the Court:

MARIFE M. LOMIBAO-CUEVAS
Clerk of Court

By:

LIBRADA C. BUENA
Division Clerk of Court, First Division

3. It is obvious that **reception** logs are records of what the COMELEC transparency server received and then broadcast last May 9, 2022, while **transmission** logs are records of what 106,174 precincts' vote counting machines individually sent to the transparency server last May 9, 2022;

4. Reception data is easy to pre-load into a Transparency Server that reports election counting results to the people. Transmission data usually leave behind many traces of its history from vote counting machines at the polling precincts thru telecommunication companies to the Transparency Server that reports election counting results to the people. If data reception time is earlier than its corresponding data transmission time then someone pre-loaded the data;

5. It appears that COMELEC either does not know the difference between reception logs and transmission logs, or, possibly, there is an attempt to mislead not only Petitioners but also the Honorable Court.

6. It is necessary and proper that such gross errors be set aright in the public interest.

PRAYER

WHEREFORE, it is respectfully prayed that the attached *Supplemental Petition* be admitted in order to supply facts which may be necessary for complete determination of the rights of the voters touching the subject matter of the Petition.

Petitioners further pray for such further and other reliefs as may be just and equitable under the premises.

Makati City for the City of Manila, April 3, 2023.

AGABIN VERZOLA & LAYAOEN
LAW OFFICE
Counsel for the Petitioners
26th Floor, Pacific Star Building
Gil Puyat Ave. cor. Makati Ave.
1200 Makati City
Tel. No. 8817-7717 • Fax No. 7751-7951
Email: averloldlaw@yahoo.com.ph

3.	It is obvious that **reception** logs are records of what the COMELEC transparency server received and then broadcast last May 9, 2022, while **transmission** logs are records of what 106,174 precincts' vote counting machines individually sent to the transparency server last May 9, 2022;

4.	Reception data is easy to pre-load into a Transparency Server that reports election counting results to the people. Transmission data usually leave behind many traces of its history from vote counting machines at the polling precincts thru telecommunication companies to the Transparency Server that reports election counting results to the people. If data reception time is earlier than its corresponding data transmission time then someone pre-loaded the data;

5.	It appears that COMELEC either does not know the difference between reception logs and transmission logs, or, possibly, there is an attempt to mislead not only Petitioners but also the Honorable Court.

6.	It is necessary and proper that such gross errors be set aright in the public interest.

PRAYER

WHEREFORE, it is respectfully prayed that the attached *Supplemental Petition* be admitted in order to supply facts which may be necessary for complete determination of the rights of the voters touching the subject matter of the Petition.

Petitioners further pray for such further and other reliefs as may be just and equitable under the premises.

Makati City for the City of Manila, April 3, 2023.

AGABIN VERZOLA & LAYAOEN
LAW OFFICE
Counsel for the Petitioners
26th Floor, Pacific Star Building
Gil Puyat Ave. cor. Makati Ave.
1200 Makati City
Tel. No. 8817-7717 • Fax No. 7751-7951
Email: *averheldlaw@yahoo.com.ph*

ooooooo

33
The Lies -Comelec is not credible – Francisco Yngente IV comments – April 2023

Hahahahaaaa Pagbukas sa mga ballot boxes, walang laman na certificate of canvass. Ang rason, na-misplaced, naiwan blah blah blah… kaya kinunan na lang ng litrato at pinadala na lang via viber? Grabe! Ang galing, napakalinis na election? What a joke!😂🕵️

Ex Estandarte - There is no perfect crime.

Masha Rostova 🏆🏆🏆 **Agent Keen**
@MashaMasha2022

Putang ina @COMELEC sagutin nyo
to...

Translate Tweet

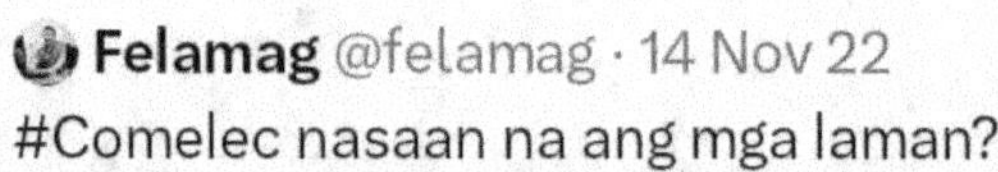

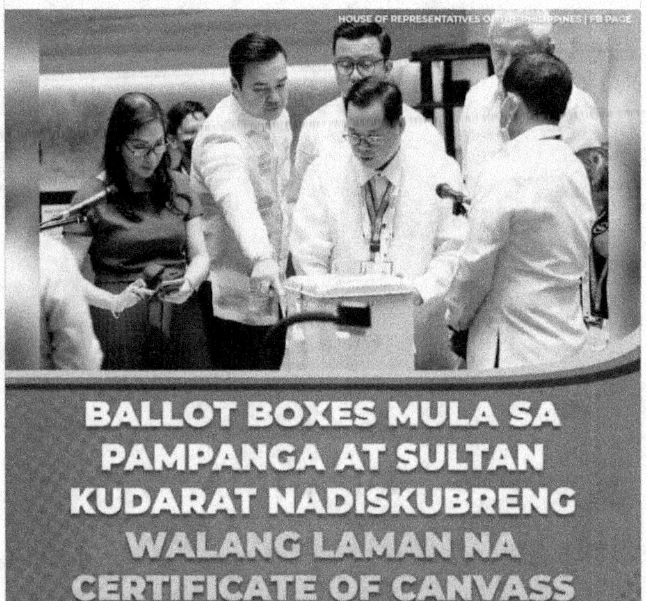

7:42 PM · 06 Apr 23 · **45.6K** Views

oooooo

REPUBLIC OF THE PHILIPPINES
SUPREME COURT
MANILA

En Banc

ELISEO MIJARES RIO JR.
AUGUSTO CADELIÑA LAGMAN
FRANKLIN FAYLOGA YSAAC,
Petitioners,

- versus -

COMMISSION ON ELECTIONS
(COMELEC)
SMARTMATIC TOTAL
INFORMATION MANAGEMENT
DITO TELECOMMUNITY
GLOBE TELECOM
SMART COMMUNICATIONS,
Respondents.

x---x

G.R. No. 263838

For: *Petition for Mandamus with Prayer for Temporary Restraining Order*

MOTION FOR LEAVE
TO FILE SUPPLEMENTAL PETITION

- -

Petitioners, thru the undersigned counsel, respectfully move to file Supplemental Petition to the instant case, and allege:

1. The COMMISSION ON ELECTIONS (Comelec) had been ignoring clamors for disclosure of election data transmission logs ever since the first request for its disclosure on 14 July 2022. When Retired Colonel Leonardo Odoño declared his intention to initiate impeachment proceedings, and more than seventy prominent military personalities signified their support for the impeachment proposal, Comelec released voluminous printouts to Colonel Odoño on 23 March 2023;

2. Upon inspection and analysis by herein Petitioners, it was discovered that what was handed to them by Respondent COMELEC were **reception** logs, instead of the requested **transmission** logs; (attached as **Annex "A"** to the *Supplemental Petition* is the Judicial Affidavit of Petitioner Gen. Eliseo M. Rio, Jr., to this effect);

REPUBLIC OF THE PHILIPPINES)
MAKATI CITY   ) S.S.

<u>VERIFIED DECLARATION</u>

I, **PACIFICO A. AGABIN**, hereby declare that the *Supplemental Petition* (and its <u>Annex "A"</u>) hereto submitted electronically in accordance with the Efficient Use of Paper Rule is complete and true copy of the documents filed with the Supreme Court.

PACIFICO A. AGABIN
Counsel
April 5, 2023

SUBSCRIBED AND SWORN TO before me this 5th day of April 2023, affiant exhibiting his competent evidence of identity, to wit: Senior Citizen ID No. 02541 issued in Marikina City on July 4, 2005.

ATTY. GERONIMO DAVID D. SITON
NOTARY PUBLIC FOR MAKATI CITY
APPT. NO. M-151 - UNTIL DEC. 31, 2023
ROLL NO. 68493 / IBCLE COMPLIANCE NO. VII-0010196/2-15-2022
IBP O.R. No. 142286 LIFETIME MEMBER MAY 5, 2017
PTR No. 9-T 9143380- JAN 02, 2023-MAKATI CITY
EXECUTIVE BLDG. CENTER MAKATI AVE., COR. JUPITER ST., MAKATI CITY

Doc. No. _44_;
Page No. _84_;
Book No. _4_;
Series of 2023.

By:

PACIFICO A. AGABIN
Roll of Attorneys No. 16609
IBP Lifetime No. 251
PTR No. MKT9569752/Jan. 10, 2023/Makati City
MCLE Exempt

Copy furnished via email:

RONNIE ADRIANO R. AMOROSO
amoroso2004@yahoo.com

GREGORIO T. MARIANO, JR., M.D.
gmarianojr@yahoo.com

Copy Furnished via courier:

COMMISSION ON ELECTIONS
8/F Palacio del Gobernador
Andres Soriano corner General Luna
Intramuros 1002 Manila

SMARTMATIC TOTAL INFORMATION MANAGEMENT
Unit 2208 22/F The Trade and Financial Tower
7th Avenue corner 32nd Street
Bonifacio Global City
1634 Taguig

ERNESTO R. ALBERTO
DITO CME Holdings President
DITO TELE COMMUNITY
21st Floor UDENNA Tower
Rizal Drive corner 4th Avenue
Bonifacio Global City 1634 Taguig

ERNEST L. CU
Globe Telecom President
GLOBE TELECOM
Globe Tower @ 2nd Street corner 7th Avenue
Bonifacio Global City 1634 Taguig

Fanklin Ysaac – April 14, 2023

Motion for Leave to File Supplemental Petition
Eliseo Mijares Rio Jr., Augusto Cadeliña Lagman,
Franklin Favloga Ysaac vs. COMELEC, et al.
<u>**G.R. No. 263838**</u>
Page | 2

3.   It is obvious that **<u>reception</u>** logs are records of what the COMELEC transparency server received and then broadcast last May 9, 2022, while **<u>transmission</u>** logs are records of what 106,174 precincts' vote counting machines individually sent to the transparency server last May 9, 2022;

4.   Reception data is easy to pre-load into a Transparency Server that reports election counting results to the people. Transmission data usually leave behind many traces of its history from vote counting machines at the polling precincts thru telecommunication companies to the Transparency Server that reports election counting results to the people. If data reception time is earlier than its corresponding data transmission time then someone pre-loaded the data;

5.   It appears that COMELEC either does not know the difference between reception logs and transmission logs, or, possibly, there is an attempt to mislead not only Petitioners but also the Honorable Court.

6.   It is necessary and proper that such gross errors be set aright in the public interest.

P R A Y E R

WHEREFORE, it is respectfully prayed that the attached *Supplemental Petition* be admitted in order to supply facts which may be necessary for complete determination of the rights of the voters touching the subject matter of the Petition.

Petitioners further pray for such further and other reliefs as may be just and equitable under the premises.

Makati City for the City of Manila, April 3, 2023.

AGABIN VERZOLA & LAYAOEN
LAW OFFICE
Counsel for the Petitioners
26th Floor, Pacific Star Building
Gil Puyat Ave. cor. Makati Ave.
1200 Makati City
Tel. No. 8817-7717 • Fax No. 7751-7951
Email: *averheldlaw@yahoo.com.ph*

t a

ooooooo

35
Don't Follow Trolls of Disinformation – Franklin Ysaac – April 14, 2023

Franklin Ysaac – April 14, 2023

My advice to followers: Don't follow trolls who specialize in disinformation.

If you are not a lawyer, stop asking questions about law . Do research and ask lawyers who are specialists in certain questions of law . If the question is about constitution, then consult a good constitutional lawyer. Don't consult a lawyer who specialize in other fields if you want to get the right answers to your question.

In medicine, would you consult a cardio if you have kidney problem ?

These trolls are only on fishing expedition . They are as guilty as fake IT who do PHISHING expedition .

So beware of these trolls who are questioning the mandamus petition. It's not useless petition. The supplemental petition is not a petition that shows lack of direction and is inconsistent with the original petition .

If you care to read or know how to read petitions, I am attaching the supplemental petition to add to your knowledge.

We are not lost in our direction. It's normal to submit supplemental petition if there is a development that is material to the original mandamus. The basis for the supplemental petition is very clear. Comelec came out with publication of transmission logs which are deemed to be reception logs not transmission logs . It's up to them to refute that in court .

As they say, " ignorance of the law is no excuse " or in Latin as I studied Latin when I was in San Jose Seminary " Ignorantia Juris non excusat ".

Please be guided accordingly.   oooooo

36
Google Surveys April 5-11, 2022 (before May 9 elections)

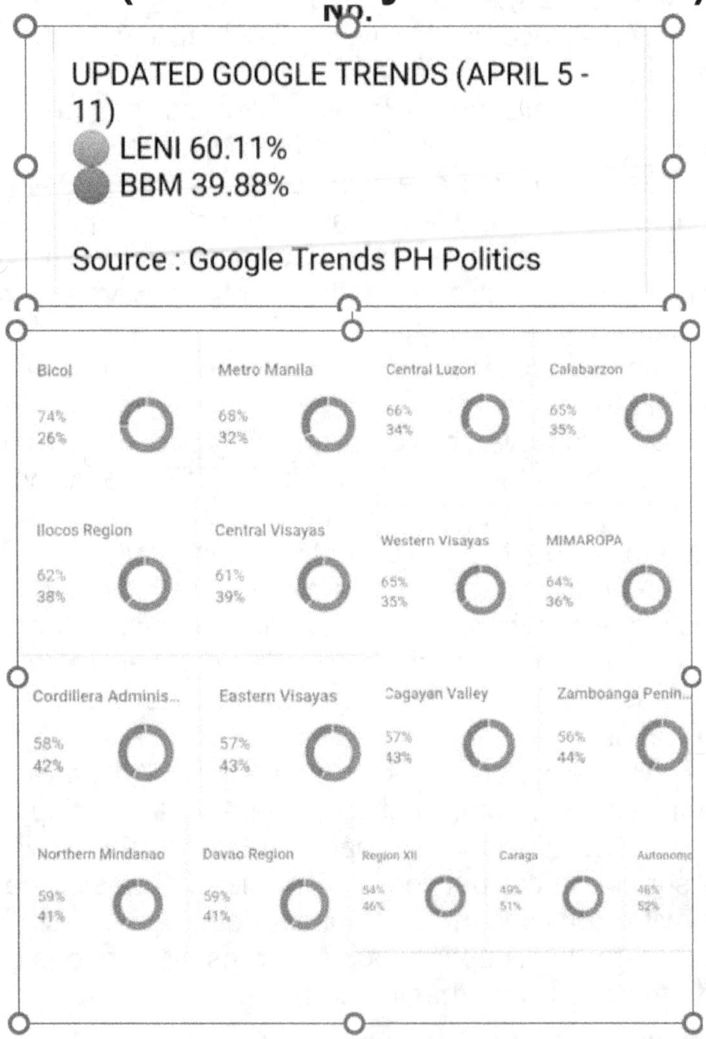

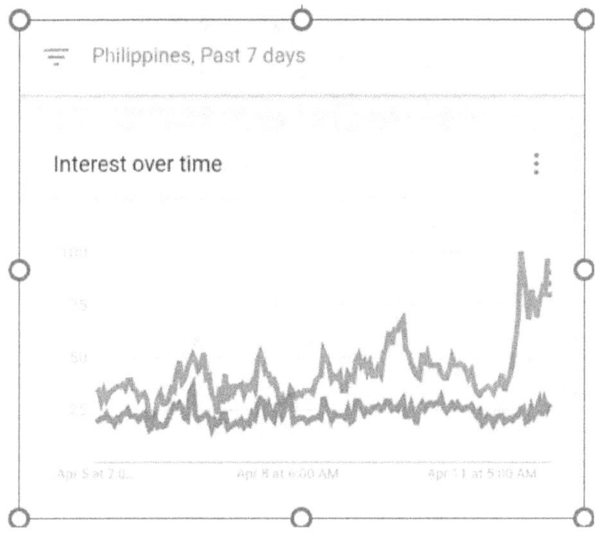
Philippines, Past 7 days
Interest over time
Apr 5 at 2:0...
Apr 8 at 6:00 AM
Apr 11 at 5:00 AM

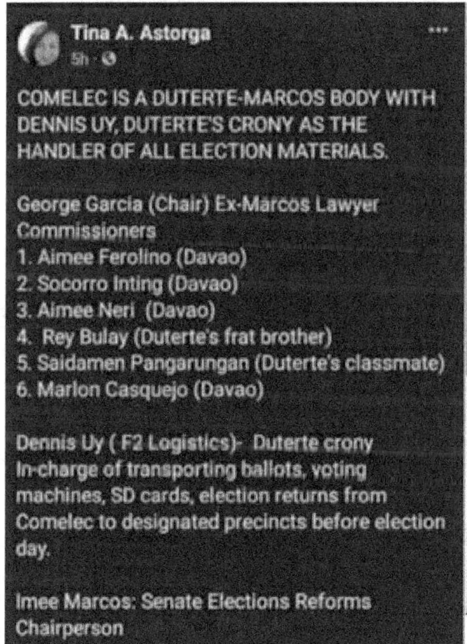
Tina A. Astorga
5h ·

COMELEC IS A DUTERTE-MARCOS BODY WITH
DENNIS UY, DUTERTE'S CRONY AS THE
HANDLER OF ALL ELECTION MATERIALS.

George Garcia (Chair) Ex-Marcos Lawyer
Commissioners
1. Aimee Ferolino (Davao)
2. Socorro Inting (Davao)
3. Aimee Neri (Davao)
4. Rey Bulay (Duterte's frat brother)
5. Saidamen Pangarungan (Duterte's classmate)
6. Marlon Casquejo (Davao)

Dennis Uy (F2 Logistics)- Duterte crony
In-charge of transporting ballots, voting
machines, SD cards, election returns from
Comelec to designated precincts before election
day.

Imee Marcos: Senate Elections Reforms
Chairperson

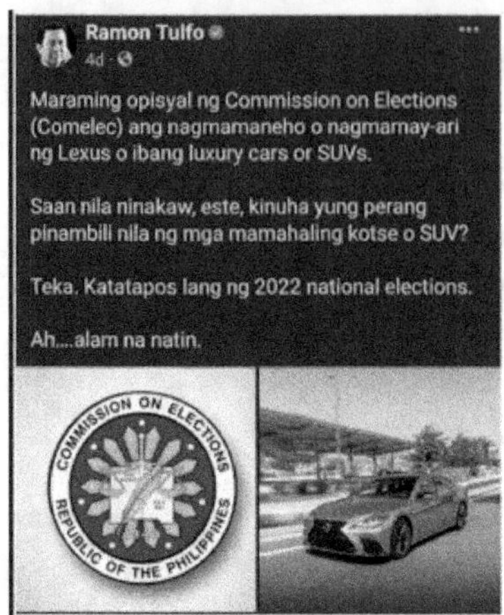

Election 2022 Survey Philippines

Gari Supena April 15, 2023

Carefully Chosen for a Fair Election 😂😂😂

Si Imee Marcos ang Chairman ng Senate Committee on Electoral Reforms and People's Participation.

Comelec Commissioners:

-Comelec Chairman Saidamen Pangarungan (Duterte appointee, Duterte schoolmate in San Beda)

-Comm. Rey Bulay (Duterte appointee, Duterte schoolmate in San Beda)

-Comm. Marlon Casquejo (Duterte appointee, origin Davao City)

-Comm. Aimee Ferolina (Duterte appointee, origin Davao City)

-Comm. Socorro Inting (Duterte appointee, origin Davao City)

-Comm. Aimee Neri (Duterte appointee, origin Davao City)

- Comm. George Garcia (known as BBM lawyer on electoral protests)

-Comelec printed more than 40 million ballots and configured SD card without witness from candidates camp representative.

-Dennis Uy (Davao businessman, Duterte crony) of F2 Logistics got a contract with Comelec to transport ballots, voting machines, SD cards, Election Returns, and other paraphernalia of Comelec to the precincts a few days before the election. - ctto

oooooo

37
Call for active support and participation -
Franklin Ysaac – April 2023

Saturday thought inspired by one of our followers

In life and in all our endeavors, we need to plan ahead . But planning needs lots of preparation . We have talents and experience and let's use them to achieve our goals .

Our goal is to find the truth . It's so elusive from the start but with IT friends who joined us in this endeavor, how can we go wrong ?

In battle preparation, we make sure we have the tools or logistics and we will need services of all who desire to achieve the same goal.

The TNTrio was just a group of three people who didn't believe in the conduct of the May election . By piecing together what we know and what we found out, we were able to solve the puzzle.

Then when we shared this with you, our followers, we opened your eyes and ears and you began to believe in us .

We can always be your leaders at the first hour but we need your time and same effort as we enjoin you to join our mandamus in court and off court.

We thank all of you for your active participation in our endeavor and we are sure the Good Lord will always be around to ensure the enemy is defeated by the truth .
Amen .

oooooo

38
Questionable "Possible" or "plain True" -
Franklin Ysaac – April 15, 2023

This is a twister ! Comelec says 20M returns " POSSIBLE". Analyze this statement. What do you conclude ?

That 20M returns is "NOT ALSO POSSIBLE".

Why ? If you have full confidence that 20M was true and correct, why make a statement it's "POSSIBLE"?

Edith Batalla
Why ask the question? They've done it! They should say "20M returns TRUE!"

oooooo

39
Class Suit of fraud – Fred Santos – April 2023

Fred Santos
It may just seem to be slap on their wrists. Combinations-- Considering its been awhile that there

has been "high probable" cause of FRAUD, there should be class suit of fraud filed by the opposition parties or the public itself to extract the transmission logs while at the same time with our legal attacks of mandamus, and people mandamus petitions. For them, maybe our mandamus petitions don't have much teeth as filing criminal fraud case has to be more scary for them.

MATINDI TALAGA ITONG COMELEC NI DUTERTE, AYAW SUMUNOD SA UTOS NG SUPREME COURT?
Kaya ba ayaw ilabas ng Comelec ang transmission logs ay dahil wala naman talagang 31M?

Comelec itigil ninyo na ang panloloko sa mga tao, ilabas ninyo na ang tunay na TRANSMISSION LOG kung wala talaga kayong maipakita maliwanag na panloloko sa mga tao ang ginawa ninyo...

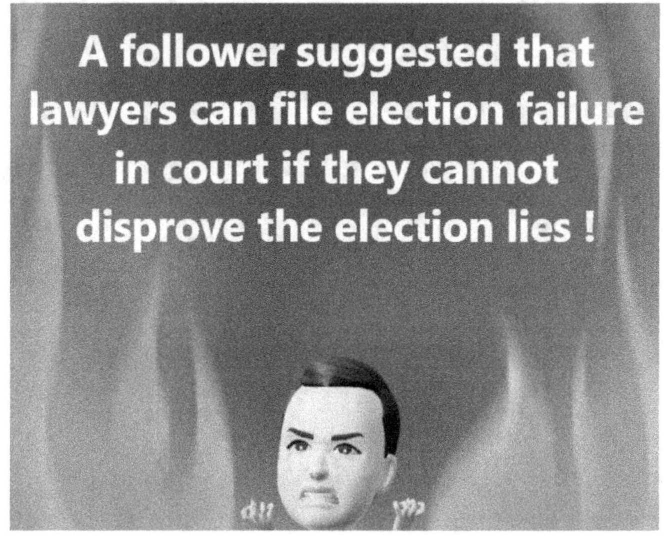

A follower suggested that lawyers can file election failure in court if they cannot disprove the election lies !

For lying about the results of the election, the authorities concerned must be held accountable for their alleged crime!

A MANIFESTO FOR TRUTH AND TRANSPARENCY

The TRUTH PETITION exhorts the COMELEC to open 750 randomly selected ballot boxes for manual counting and audit of SD cards.

We aim to get 2 million signatures from Filipinos worldwide.

bit.ly/TruthPetitionPH
@TruthPetitionPH

> **80% & 84% approval rates of Marcos & Duterte respectively! Rarely does any US President get this rating, not even the BEST of the presidents! STOP all survey machines of deception!**

ooooooo

40

DIRECT EVIDENCE THAT THE 2022 ELECTION WAS RIGGED. - Eliseo Rio Jr – posted by LIBERAL PARTY (LP) - Regina Sy-Facunda Dy Seng - April 21, 2023

This proof of fraudulent data came from the"List of VCM Received May 9, 2022 NLE" that COMELEC itself uploaded in its website. How could three clustered precincts have exactly the same number of actual voters of an unbelievable 1,000 people, immediately followed by a precinct with 0 voter? How could an official document of COMELEC contain so many anomalies (we have shown and will show more irregularities where ERs of precincts were received by the Transparency Server even HOURS BEFORE these ERs were transmitted by the VCMs) be considered the result of a clean and honest election?

LIST OF VCM RECEIVED MAY 9, 2022 NLE

NO.	CLUSTERED	ACTUAL	RECEPTION DATETIME
105951	39141532	593	11-May-2022 15:54:40
105952	39141533	416	11-May-2022 15:56:44
105953	39141504	482	11-May-2022 15:58:43
105954	36070018	439	11-May-2022 15:59:52
105955	39101368	278	11-May-2022 16:01:25
105956	92120282	0	11-May-2022 16:02:27
105957	39141511	453	11-May-2022 16:03:15
105958	36070006	655	11-May-2022 16:18:21
105959	36070014	3	11-May-2022 16:32:21
105960	92120253	1,000	11-May-2022 17:19:39
105961	92120230	1,000	11-May-2022 17:21:34
105962	92120232	1,000	11-May-2022 17:23:09
105963	92120275	0	11-May-2022 17:24:27
105964	66120038	3	11-May-2022 17:44:51
105965	36120032	324	11-May-2022 17:58:26
105966	38100034	528	11-May-2022 18:01:45
105967	38280033	445	11-May-2022 18:09:22
105968	07010125	434	11-May-2022 18:17:12

ooooooo

41
Lead Counsel Atty. Agabin Statement- Franklin Ysaac – April 22, 2023

In the interview last night with our lead counsel, Atty Agabin by Mike Apacible, the medium was choppy, but the message was clear:

No matter what the respondents do to delay or what the SC may do to dismiss the mandamus, no government authority can thumb down a case based on constitutional ground, a voters right to know about his vote from the time he cast his vote, to counting, transmission and to knowing whether his or her vote was really counted.

To deny such constitutional right is a travesty of the very democratic right and existence of a real government whose task is to preserve not only the election data but the integrity of an honest, transparent election process which is the only time the voters can voice their choice of their true leaders.

Throughout history of nations, no authority coming from leaders elected illegitimately can last as eventually, the voices of the voters and the People will learn about the truth whether the election was fraudulent or not.

If the mandamus case is thrown out for unconstitutional reasons like the usual that the case is without any merit or the case is beyond the court's jurisdiction is a betrayal of public trust and the people can exercise their voices outside the court and justice can be served if the truth finally becomes known to all and the people must rise to protect the truth.

Let no government authority trample on this very right which is exercised by the people only during election period. If the people's rights are trampled then that's the end of democracy and like many illegitimate governments, they eventually fall as people cannot accept they have been duped !

The fight for truth must continue and as what the ancient Greeks would do when they seek the wrath of Zeus to punish the wicked "He sends them to Tartarus, the Greek version of hell-an abyss where the wicked are subjected to divine punishment".

Our Christian God is less severe. He knows what bad things you do to His people and He gives you all the chances to reform, do restitution and penance as He alone can subject you to punishment while here on earth or in the next life.

Don't fail Him and if you don't trust the Merciful God, then He will make His judgment in many ways which may be immediate or gradual.

I have seen His judgment from my personal experience and from what I have witnessed.

You have seen and witnessed too how our benevolent God has His limits too.

Don't test Him as we ask the guilty parties who try to hide their crimes they still have time unless they are not afraid or they can accept their own Comeuppance !!!

oooooo

42

Deceptive Results in 2022 Election Must be Exposed and punished - Franklin Ysaac – April 22, 2023

I didn't realize my early posts about my concerns on the early results coming from transparency server to go viral.

I was just voicing my suspicious mind and just like everyone else, I have expressed my doubts and am staring and crying in disbelief that even before the voters were able to cast their ballots, results about 57 pct have already gone to BBM. I couldn't take this sitting down.

Hence, since I am partly familiar with smartmatic operation since I was a consultant to a satellite provider for areas without internet connection during the last election, this transparency result deserves scrutiny from IT experts.

Reactions voiced by those who read my post are already claiming this has been hacked or rigged.

Immediately what came to my mind is that there is possibility that this transparency server has already been pre programmed. What is obvious to the operator of this transparency is he or they think that by releasing the result way ahead before the last votes are in, they can manipulate the minds of the people that the election is over.

My suspicious mind began to work that there is probability there are two or more servers independent of real transparency server. Normally, as IT provider, we provide mirror for database just in case the main server malfunctions . In short, the transparency server is the last resort and it cannot be the main unless the real server fails.

Now, with PPCRV doing the ER count, where do these ER go if the transparency server says it's 97 pct complete. So, PPCRV is useless because what they are doing may not validate the transparency figure.

As a solution, I mentioned that access to the transparency server and getting source data which are ER is first step . Then share these data with PPCRV to check the veracity of actual ERs being encoded versus transparency source data. If there are huge discrepancies, then we need to get to the bottom of this.

Who encoded the false source data in transparency server ?

This can be determined as there are log in data in transparency server ?

Long and tedious but we have to do our job as many Filipinos are beginning to lose faith again in our electoral process .

There were some who commented that did big money change hands ? I have no evidence on that .

But I like to thank those who made comments about praying for our tasks and some even offering monetary considerations which I immediately turned down.

Nobody asked me why I was doing this.

My simple answer is this - if we close our eyes to anomalies like this being committed, then who will stop them. Election system will be like this again and again.

Should we go back to manual then?

No. There are safeguards and rail guards to thwart attempts to hacking .

As a former banker, we invest heavily on cyber security systems and every year we update our security systems .

I can't write about security systems now but there are providers who are credible and in the future, Comelec should get these systems working.

Otherwise, the current system is useless and we will have this hacking, rigging forever to win election.

May God forbid this from happening and May the TRUTH be our strength !

ooooooo

43
The Rigging of Philippine National Election 2022 - Christina Astorga, Ph.D.
– April 23, 2023

THE RIGGING OF PHILIPPINE NATIONAL ELECTION 2022

COMELEC Duped the Nation and the Nation was Cheated

Christina Astorga, Ph.D.

Isinalin sa Filipino ni Dr. Ason Hipolito (Mag - scroll pababa)

When the Philippine national election 2022 ended with Ferdinand Marcos, Jr. and Sara Duterte winning overwhelmingly over the Opposition, and VP Leni declaring her defeat, finding no evidence of election fraud, based on the advice of her lawyers, the lights went out for all democracy fighters. It was the end of the road, and the beginning of another Marcos regime, with Sara Duterte as VP who is already poised to take over the reins after six years, and perhaps a son of Marcos, or a sibling of Duterte to follow her.

A dark scenario to reckon with, until three wise men appeared on the scene, who, following the star of truth, exposed the election fraud. They called themselves TNTrio—the acronym TNT, standing for Truth and Transparency, and Trio, referring to three Information Technology experts who ripped into the election fraud behind the landslide win of Marcos-Duterte. They have formidable credentials: Retired General Brigadier Eliseo M. Rio, Jr. was a former Chairman of the National TeleCommunications Commission and the former secretary of the Department of Information and Communications Technology. He was also the Group Commander of the Technical Intelligence Group (MIG21) of ISAFP, and the former Chair of the COMELEC Advisory Council. Mr. Augusto C. Lagman was one of the pioneers of Systems Technology Institute (STI) and former President of the Philippine Computer Society. He was a former Commissioner of the COMELEC and served as Chairman and President of Namfrel for four decades. Mr. Franklin F.Ysaac is the President of the Franklin Fnancials Consultancy, Phil.Inc. and was the President of FINEX (Financial Executive Institute of the Philippines) in 2004. Confluence of events brought these three wise men, who did not know each other personally, together at the same side of the battlefield, fighting for the same cause—the truth and integrity of the Philippine National Election of 2022.

The TNTRio questioned the 20 million+ votes shown to the public as counted by the Transparency Server at 8:02 after the polls closed at 7 p.m. COMELEC General Instructions (GI) Resolution 10762 promulgated on February 16, 2022 for the May 9, 2022 Election required 9 major tasks to be done by the Election Board before transmitting the precinct's ER (Election Return) after the voting closed. The time required to accomplish all these 9 tasks, the longest of which is the printing of eight copies of the ER (Election Return) is around 19 minutes, based on the official COMELEC Hands-On Lecture Demo Video of VCM (Voting Counting Machine) operations for the 2022 Election, as contrary to the 8 minutes COMELEC said it took before the VCM transmissions started. COMELEC is clearly contradicting its own Demo Video.

Just an hour after voting closed at 7 p.m., Retired General Brigadier Rio, Jr., or Sir Rio from hereon, said that "an incredible 20M+ votes were counted, the highest number of votes ever counted in the first hour in our election history, if not in the whole world. And in that hour, from 7 p.m. to 8 p.m., the earliest transmissions of ERs (Election Returns) could only occur by 7:19, making that record breaking count of 20M+ in just 41 minutes! And as astounding is that in the second hour, from 8 p.m., the votes counted unexplainably dropped to just 13.2+ votes when all tasks required in the GI (General Instructions) would have been done on the first hour."

While millions were not able to vote, the election of the President and Vice President was "fait accompli" in that first hour alone, as what followed in a four-day counting period, was this uncanny vote ratios for all candidates for Presidency and VP that hardly changed. Sir Rio said that "such results can only be programmed, and whoever manipulated the TS (Transparency Server) results knew what the "official" results of the election will be even before counting began."

COMELEC said that the incredible speed of election returns was largely because they were successful in setting up the system for speed. The TNTRio, however, were not questioning the fast rate of the VCM transmissions from the precincts as this can be done with technology as we have now, but what was incredulous to them was the exact time the fast rate of transmissions started at 7:08 P.M, after the polls closed at 7 p.m., for it was impossible as aforementioned, as it takes at least 19 minutes for all the administrative matters required by COMELEC to be completed before any transmission can start. But what is more astounding if not alarming is that the votes being counted by the Transparency Server in that first hour were more than what the VCMS from the precincts were transmitting, when this process is synchronized to the minutest second. This was exposed by COMELEC itself when the Chair showed the actual accumulated VCM transmissions to the public on Oct. 18, 2022, at a forum sponsored by the Ateneo de Manila University, in which they themselves got their hands caught in the cookie jar.

COMELEC's Oct. 18, 2022 graph showed that VCM transmissions peaked at the second hour after transmissions started, which diametrically is in conflict with the Transparency Count that peaked in the first hour in their March 23, 2023 graph, where at 8:02 an incredible 20 M+ votes were counted by the Transparency Server, when only 12M+ votes were transmitted at the same time by the VCM. The Transparency Server was counting 8 M votes more than what the VCMS were transmitting which is indubitably fraudulent. The Transparency Server was fabricating votes in the first hour of counting to establish firmly the landslide win of Marcos and Duterte. IF Parish Pastoral Council for Responsible Voting (PPCRV) and the NAMFREL-LENTE's Random Manual Audit (RMA) in their parallel count validated the COMELEC count, it is because they were basing their count on the same fabricated data. They became involuntary accomplices of the COMELEC fraud .

TNTRio posed two challenges to COMELEC. First, that COMELEC was to demonstrate in public how their system can accomplish all the Election requirements in 8 minutes against 19 minutes before any VCM can transmit. Second, that COMELEC publish the transparency data that were the basis of the "Accumulated VCM Transmissions" graph that COMELEC presented to the public, where it showed that the Transparency Server peaked at 20 M votes in the first hour, when the VCM count only transmitted 12M in the same first hour. The COMELEC failed to meet both challenges. After 6 months of waiting for COMELEC to publish the transmission logs, the TNTRio filed a Mandamus petition to the SC to compel COMELEC to abide by its constitutional duty to transparency and truth. SC gave COMELEC ten days to meet the Mandamus, which they failed to do.

If COMELEC has the transmission logs of the 20M+, they would have immediately published them. Apparently they did not have them, because what they submitted, on March 23,2023, to Sir Rio and Ret. Colonel Leonardo Odono, who declared that he was going to file an impeachment case against 5 COMELEC Commissioners in Congress, were not transmission logs but reception logs. This further eroded the credibility of COMELEC and exacerbated the growing suspicion that it systematically duped the nation. Did COMELEC really have those 20M votes?

In the Public Online Forum on April 15, "Ano ang Kabuluhan ng Pandaraya sa Election at ng Mandamus Case sa Buhay Mo?" Sir Rio presented DIRECT EVIDENCE of fraud, beyond the preponderance of circumstantial evidence, using physical evidence of data which COMELEC itself uploaded on its site, which it deceitfully said were transmission logs but were actually reception logs. In his presentation, Sir Rio showed how the Transparency Server posted ER (Election Return) before they were even transmitted by the VCM precincts. There was one case when the Transparency Server posted ER 2 hours even before VCM transmitted them. How can the Transparency Server show what it has not yet received, except that it was pre-loaded.

The latest vlog of Maharlika, a former BFF of Lisa Marcos, an insider of the Marcos inner circle, who has turned into a whistle blower, confirms TNTRio's observations that Election 2022 was rigged. In the video clip showing the conversation between Lisa and Maharlika on May 8, a day before the election, Lisa already knew what the results of the election will be. To make up for some thing that went awry about Maharlika's ticket to the "Miting de Avance" which made Maharlika angry, Lisa invited her to an undisclosed location to witness a "secret counting session like a PPCRV" at 7 p.m. of May 9, after voting has closed, where Maharlika can make a scoop of the winning of BBM which she can post on her vlog by 9 p.m. of May 9.

Sir Rio posted the searing question: "Why was Lisa so sure that BBM would have won by 9 PM as of May 9, a day before the Election? Why was she so sure that she even offered this event as an exclusive "gift" to make up with Maharlika? How could she have predicted the Transparency Server Results shown to the public in those two hours after voting closed would be favorable to her husband? Madame Lisa, is this what you did last summer?"

The answer to this question is TNTRIO's declaration that "the results of the Transparency Server were statistically, mathematically, and logically highly improbable, if not impossible. Whoever manipulated the Transparency Server results knew what the "official" results of the election will be even BEFORE counting began."

COMELEC duped the nation and the nation was duped. Senator Lee Rhiannon, Commissioner of the Philippine Election 2022 International Observer Mission declared: "The evidence is overwhelming… Marcos Jr. and Sara Duterte were not elected legitimately."

ANG PANDARAYA SA PAMBANSANG HALALAN 2022 NG PILIPINAS

COMELEC Niloko ang Bansa at ang Bansa ay Nadaya

By Christina Astorga, Ph.D.

Isinalin sa Filipino ni Dr. Ason Hipolito

Nang matapos ang Pambansang Halalan 2022 ng Pilipinas na si Ferdinand Marcos, Jr. at Sara Duterte ang nanalo ng may napakalaking lamang sa Opposition, at dineklara ni VP Leni ang kanyang pagkatalo dahil walang ebidensiya ng pandaraya, ayon sa kanyang mga abogado, nagdilim ang kapaligiran para sa lahat ng mga lumalaban para sa demokrasya. Animo'y iyon na ang katapusan ng daan, at ang panibagong yugto ng rehimeng Marcos, na may naka-ambang Sara Duterte na hahalili pagkaraan ng anim (6) na taon, o marahil isa sa mga anak ni Marcos Jr., o isa sa mga kapatid ni Duterte ang susunod sa kanya.

Isang malagim na pangitain, hanggang may Tatlong Mago na dumating sa eksena, na sumusunod sa Tala ng Katotohanan, at ibinulgar ang pandaraya sa halalan. Sila ay binansagang TNTrio – ang acronym na TNT ay para sa TRUTH and TRANSPARENCY, at Trio para sa tatlong (3) Information Technology experts na naglantad sa pandarayang nagbigay-daan sa nakamamanghang panalo ng Marcos-Duterte tandem. Sila ay armado ng mabibigat na credentials: Si Retired BGen. Eliseo M. Rio Jr. ay naging Chairman ng National TeleCommunications Commission at Kalihim ng Department of Information and Communications Technology, at kasabayang nagsilbing Chairman ng COMELEC Advisory Council. Ilang taon din siyang nagsilbi bilang miyembro at Commander ng Technical Intelligence Group (MIG21) ng Intelligence Service of the Armed Forces of the Philippines (ISAFP). Si Mr. Augusto C. Lagman ay isa sa mga nagtayo ng Systems Technology Institute (STI) at naging Presidente ng Philippine Computer Society. Siya ay naging Commissioner ng COMELEC, at nakapagsilbi din bilang miyembro, Chairman at Presidente ng National Citizens' Movement for Free Elections (NAMFREL) ng halos apat na dekada. Si Mr. Franklin F. Ysaac ay ang Presidente ng Franklin Financials Consultancy Phils., Inc. at naging Presidente ng Financial Executive Institute of the Philippines (FINEX) noong 2004. Ang pagdaloy ng mga pangyayari ang naging dahilan na magtagpo ang mga hindi magkaka-kilalang tatlong mago sa isang panig ng digmaan para sa isang adhikain – ang katotohanan at integridad ng Pambansang Halalan 2022 ng Pilipinas.

Ang TNTrio ay nag-duda sa 20+ milyong boto na ipinakita sa publiko ng Transparency Server nang 8:02pm, pagkatapos magsarado ang mga presinto ng 7:00pm. Ipinahayag ng COMELEC General Instructions (GI), Resolution 10762 noong Pebrero 16, 2022 na para sa halalan ng Mayo 09, 2022, pagkatapos isara ang botohan, kinakailangan munang maisagawa ang siyam (9) na pangunahing tungkulin ng Election Board bago mag-umpisa ng transmission ng Election Returns (ER). Ang oras na gugugulin para matapos ang 9 na tungkulin ay humigit-kumulang na labing-siyam (19) na minutos, na ang pinakamatagal gawin ay ang pag-imprenta ng walong kopya ng ER, ayon sa opisiyal na COMELEC Hands-On Lecture Demo Video of VCM (Vote Counting Machine) operations for the 2022 Elections, na salungat sa walong minutos na sinabi ng COMELEC na magugugol bago mag-umpisa ang VCM transmission. Maliwanag na sinasalungat ng COMELEC ang kanila mismong Demo Video.

Makaraan pa lamang ng isang oras pagkasarado ng botohan ng 7:00pm, sinabi ni Ret. BGen. Rio Jr. (Sir

Rio) na "ang kaduda-dudang 20+ milyong boto na nabilang na, at ito'y masasabing pinaka-mataas ng bilang ng boto na naitala sa unang oras sa buong kasaysayan ng halalan sa Pilipinas, kung hindi man sa buong mundo. At sa unang oras, mula 7:00pm hanggang 8:00pm, ang pinaka-maagang transmission ng ERs ay maaari lang mangyari ng bandang 7:19pm, kaya record-breaker ang 20+ milyong boto sa loob ng 41 minutos! At katulad rin ng nakakamanghang ikalawang oras, mula 8:00pm, ang mga botong nabilang ay bumagsak sa di-maipaliwanag na 13.2+ milyong boto, gayong sa oras na ito, lahat ng tungkuling hinihingi ng General Instructions ay nairaos na sa unang oras".

Habang may ilang milyon ang hindi pa nakakaboto, ang pagkaka-halal sa Presidente at Bise-Presidente, sa unang oras pa lamang, ay matuturing na fait accompli, dahil sa sumunod na apat (4) na araw ng bilangan, mayroong nakapagtatakang vote-ratio na hindi nag-iiba para sa lahat ng mga kandidato para sa Presidente at Bise-Presidente. Ayon kay Sir Rio na "ang gayong resulta ay nai-programa na, at kung sinuman ang nagmanipula sa resulta ng Transparency Server ay batid na ang "official results" ng halalan, bago pa man nag-umpisa ang bilangan".

Ayon sa COMELEC, ang nakakamanghang bilis ng transmission ng Election Returns ay dahil matagumpay nilang naisa-ayos ang sistema para sa bilis. Kaya lang, hindi ang mabilis na VCM transmissions ang kinukuwestiyon ng TNTrio, dahil sa makabagong teknolohiya ay possible talaga iyon, kundi ang hindi kapani-paniwalang eksaktong oras na nag-umpisa ang mabilis na transmission, na 7:08pm, makatapos magsarado ng 7:00pm, dahil sa nabanggit nang ka-imposiblehan na aabutin ng 19 na minutos para matapos ang mga tungkuling hinihingi ng COMELEC bago mag-umpisa ang transmission. Ngunit ang mas nakakagulat, kundi man nakakabahala, ay ang mga botong nabilang ng Transparency Server sa unang oras ay higit pa kaysa sa bilang na nata-transmit ng VCMs mula sa mga botohang presinto, gayong ang oras ng lahat ng mga proseso ay magkakasabay sa pinaka-maiksing segundo. COMELEC mismo ang nag-buko sa sarili nila nang ang kanilang Chairman ay nagpakita ng "Accumulated VCM Transmissions" graph sa publiko noong Oktubre 18, 2022, sa isang forum sa Ateneo de Manila University.

Pinakita ng COMELEC graph ng Okt.18 na ang VCM transmissions ay nag-rurok ng ikalawang oras mula nang mag-umpisa ang transmissions, at hindi tumutugma sa Transparency Server kung saan nagrurok sa unang oras sa kanilang Marso 23, 2023 graph, kung saan nang 8:02pm ang kaduda-dudang 20+ milyong boto ay nabilang ng Transparency Server, habang 12+ milyong boto lamang ang na-transmit ng mga VCMs sa parehong panahon. Ang Transparency Server ay nagbilang ng higit 8 milyong boto kaysa sa tina-transmit ng VCMs at ito ay walang alinlangang pandaraya. Ang Transparency Server ay nag-imbento ng mga boto sa unang oras ng bilangan para lang maitatag ang kamangha-manghang panalo nina Marcos at Duterte. Kung ang Parish Pastoral Council for Responsible Voting (PPCRV) at ang NAMFREL-LENTE Random Manual Audit (RMA), sa kanilang "parallel count" ay naipagtibay ang COMELEC count, iyon ay sa kadahilanang ang mga binilang nila ay nakabatay sa parehong inimbentong datos. Sila ay mga di-sadyang kasabwat sa pandaraya ng COMELEC.

Nagkasa ng dalawang hamon ang TNTrio sa COMELEC. Una, ipakita ng COMELEC sa publiko kung paano matatapos lahat ng hinihinging tungkulin sa loob ng 8 minutos laban sa 19 minutos, bago mag-umpisang mag-transmit ang mga VCMs. Ikalawa, ilabas ng COMELEC ang transparency data na siyang batayan ng "Accumulated VCM Transmissions" graph na kanilang ipinakita sa publiko, kung saan nagrurok ng 20+ milyong boto ang Transparency Server sa unang oras, habang ang VCM count ay 12+ milyong boto lang ang na-transmit sa parehong unang oras. Nabigo ang COMELEC na harapin ang 2 paghamon. Makaraan ang anim na buwang paghihintay para ilabas ng COMELEC ang transmission logs, dumulog ang TNTrio sa Korte Suprema para sa isang Petition for Mandamus upang utusan ang COMELEC na tumupad sa kanilang obligasyon ayon sa Constitution na maging tapat at makatotohanan. Binigyan ng Korte Suprema ang COMELEC ng sampung (10) araw upang tumugon sa Mandamus, ngunit bigo pa rin sila.

Kung ang COMELEC ay hawak ang transmission logs ng 20+Milyong boto, hindi ba madaling ipakita kaagad ang mga iyon? Tila wala silang transmission logs dahil ang ibinigay nila noong Marso 23, 2023 kay Ret. Col. Odoño, na nagbantang maghahain ng Impeachment Case laban sa limang (5) COMELEC Commissioners, at kay Sir Rio, ay hindi transmission logs kundi mga reception logs. Mas lalo nitong nasira ang kredibilidad ng COMELEC at pinalala ang lumalaking paghihinala na sistematikong dinaya nila ang bansa. Mayroon ba talagang hawak na transmission logs ang COMELEC para sa 20+milyong boto?

Sa public online Forum noong Abril 15 na "Ano Ang Kabuluhan ng Pandaraya sa Election at ng Mandamus Case sa Buhay Mo?," iprinisenta ni Sir Rio ang DIREKTANG EBIDENSIYA ng pandaraya, lagpas pa sa kasaganaan ng circumstantial evidence, gamit ang mga kinatawang datos na COMELEC mismo ang naglabas sa kanilang website, at mapanlinlang na sinabing transmission logs ang mga reception logs. Naipakita ni Sir Rio kung paano natanggap ng Transparency Server ang ER sa ganitong oras bago pa man naitransmit ng VCM ang datos mula sa presinto. May isang insidente na natanggap ng Transparency Server ang ER dalawang (2) oras bago pa man na-transmit ng VCM ang ER. Paanong masasabi na may natanggap ang Transparency Server ng datos na hindi pa nata-transmit, puwera na lang kung ito ay kargado na ng mga boto bago pa man nagbotohan.

Sa isang vlog ni Maharlika, isang dating matalik na kaibigan ni Lisa Marcos at insider sa Marcos circle, ngunit naging whistle-blower, kinumpirma niya ang mga napansing pandaraya ng TNTrio ukol sa Halalan 2022. Sa video-clip na pinaparinig ang usapan ng dalawa nung Mayo 08, isang araw bago ng halalan, alam na ni Lisa kung ano ang magiging resulta ng halalan. Para makabawi sa ikinagalit ni Maharlika tungkol sa kanyang ticket sa Miting de Avance, inimbitahan siya ni Lisa na pumunta ng Mayo 09 sa ganap na 7:00pm sa isang lihim na lugar para mapanood niya ang isang "secret counting session like a PPCRV", para makagawa siya ng scoop sa pagkakapanalo ni BBM, ngunit bandang 9:00pm na lang niya ipapakita sa kanyang online vlog.

Ito ang nagbabagang tanong ni Sir Rio: "Bakit isang araw bago ng halalan ay siguradong-sigurado si Lisa na mananalo si BBM pagtuntong ng 9:00pm ng Mayo 09? Bakit siya siguradong-sigurado at ginawa pang piling handog ang session na iyon para makabawi kay Maharlika? Paano niya nahulaan na sa unang 2 oras ng bilangan, ang Transparency Server results na napapanood ng publiko ay aayon para sa kanyang mister? Madame Lisa, ito ba ang ginawa mo nang summer ng 2022?"

Ang sagot sa mga katanungang ito ay ang pahayag ng TNTrio na "ang resulta ng Transparency Server ay malayong mangyari, kundi man imposible, ayon sa siyensiya ng Statistics, Mathematics at Logic. Kung sinuman ang nagmanipula ng Transparency Server results ay alam na niya ang "official results" ng halalan bago pa man nag-umpisa ang bilangan.

Niloko ng COMELEC ang bansa at ang bansa ay nadaya. Ang dating Australian Senator Lee Rhiannon, Commissioner ng International Observer Mission ay nagpahayag tungkol sa Halalan 2022 na "Ang ebidensiya ay katakut-takot….Marcos Jr. at Sara Duterte ay hindi nahalal ng lehitimong paraan."

oooooo

44
Comelec and SC are deceiving the public – Eliseo Rio Jr. – April 23, 2023

COMELEC is deceiving not only the voting public but EVEN the Supreme Court (SC). On January 10, 2023, the SC En Banc required a respondent COMELEC among others to comment on our "Petition for Mandamus with prayer for Temporary Restraining Order (TRO) to Compel Preservation and/or Restrain Alteration/Erasure/Deletion of Subscriber and Cyber Traffic Data Integrity of Telecom Transmission of National Election Results from 7pm to at Least 9pm of May 9, 2022 Philippine Time".

To this COMELEC, through the Solicitor General, answered on April 3, 2023, as shown on page 4 of their letter response, that they have published on March 22, 2023 the "Received VCM Transmission" and by publishing the "transmission logs", our petition was made moot. But what they published are ACTUALLY Reception Logs that can be easily altered, BUT what was being petitioned is the preservation and non-alteration of TELECOM TRANSMISSIONS.

COMELEC WOULD LIKE TO MAKE THE SUPREME COURT AND THE FILIPINO PEOPLE BELIEVE THAT TRANSMISSION LOGS ARE THE SAME AS RECEPTION LOGS. AND THE RECEPTION LOGS SHOWN BY COMELEC HAVE MANY ANOMALOUS DATA.

To simplify matters, during the October 18, 2022 forum, when COMELEC was bragging that the May 9, 2022 elections were the best elections ever, Comelec Chairman George Garcia promised to allow the telcos to disclose the truth to the people. We ask the Comelec Chairman to honor his own promise. ALLOW THE TELCOS TO DISCLOSE THE TRUTH!

Supreme Court
Baguio City

EN BANC

NOTICE

Sirs/Mesdames:

Please take notice that the Court en banc issued a Resolution dated **JANUARY 10, 2023,** *which reads as follows:*

"**G.R. No. 263838** (Eliseo Mijares Rio, Jr., Augusto Cadeliña Lagman and Franklin Fayloga Ysaac vs. Commission on Elections, Smartmatic Total Information Management, DITO Telecommunity, Globe Telecom, and Smart Communications).- The Court Resolved to **IMPLEAD** the Joint Congressional Oversight Committee on Automated Election System (JCOC) and the Commission on Elections (COMELEC) Advisory Council (CAC) as respondents.

Acting on the 'Petition for Mandamus with Prayer for Temporary Restraining Order (TRO) to Compel Preservation and/or Restrain Alteration/Erasure/Deletion of Subscriber and Cyber Traffic Data Integrity of Telecom Transmissions of National Election Results from 7pm to at Least 9pm of May 9, 2022 Philippines Time,' the Court Resolved, without giving due course to the petition, to

(a)   **REQUIRE** respondents COMELEC, JCOC and CAC to **COMMENT** on the petition and prayer for TRO and/or injunction within ten (10) days from notice hereof; and

(b)   **REQUIRE** the petitioners to **COMPLY**, within five (5) days from notice hereof, with the following procedural requirements:

(i)   requirement to submit proper verification pursuant to Section 5, Rule 64, in relation to Section 4, Rule 7, 1997 Rules of Civil Procedure, as amended, it appearing that the attestations in the verification are incomplete;

(ii)   requirement to submit proper proof of service (*e.g.*, a written admission of the party served, or an affidavit of the party serving and registry receipts) of the petition on the adverse parties pursuant to Section 5, Rule 64 in relation to Section 17, Rule 13, same Rules, it appearing

---

COMMENT
Rio, Jr., et al. v. COMELEC, et al.
G.R. No. 263838
x------------------------------------x

4.   On 22 March 2023, the COMELEC released and uploaded in its official website the List of VCM Transmission Logs of the 9 May 2022 national and local elections. The COMELEC uploaded not only the files containing the "List of VCM Received During First Hour of Transmission May 9, 2022 NLE" which petitioners seek to be preserved, but also the "List of VCM Received Entire Transmission Logs May 9, 2022 NLE."[8] The decision to make the data publicly available was to erase doubts on the credibility of the automated election system. With the publication of the transmission logs, the public can access more information regarding the election process, essential to guaranteeing accountability and transparency in the country's electoral system.

5.   Plainly, the present Petition for *Mandamus* is dismissible on the ground of mootness. A case becomes "moot" when it ceases to present a justiciable controversy by supervening events so that a declaration thereon would be of no practical use or value. Here, the publication of the transmission logs of the 9 May 2022 national and local Elections has rendered the Petition moot and *academic*.

6.   A case becomes moot when there is no more actual controversy between the parties or no useful purpose can be served in passing upon the merits. Courts will not determine a moot question in a case in which no practical relief can be granted. It is unnecessary to indulge in academic discussion of a case presenting a moot question, as a judgment thereon cannot have any practical legal effect or, in the nature of things, cannot be enforced.[9]

7.   In *Garcia v. COMELEC*,[10] this Honorable Court held that where the issues have become moot and academic, there is no justiciable controversy, thereby rendering the resolution of the same of no practical use or value.

8.   Similarly, in *Gancho-on v. Secretary of Labor and Employment*,[11] this Honorable Court ruled that:

---

[8] https://comelec.gov.ph/?r=2022NLE/VCM_2022NLE_TRANSMISSION_LOGS last accessed on March 24, 2023; copies of the Certifications from the COMELEC are likewise attached as Annexes "A" and "B".
[9] *Baldo v. COMELEC, et al.*, G.R. No. 176135, June 16, 2009.
[10] 328 Phil. 288 (1996).
[11] 337 Phil. 654, 658 (1997).

000000